The Start-Up Junkie's Playbook

The Start-Up Junkie's Playbook

A 30-Step Plan to Launch Your Business

Jay J. Silverberg

BEP

BUSINESS EXPERT PRESS

Leader in applied, concise business books

The Start-Up Junkie's Playbook: A 30-Step Plan to Launch Your Business

First published in 2023 by
Business Expert Press, LLC
222 East 46th Street, New York, NY 10017
www.businessexpertpress.com

ISBN-13: 978-1-63742-526-8 (paperback)
ISBN-13: 978-1-63742-527-5 (e-book)

Business Expert Press Entrepreneurship and Small Business Management Collection

First edition: 2023

10 9 8 7 6 5 4 3 2 1

To all you newbie entrepreneurs, and you would-bes, wannabes, and tire kickers, I have often been on that business start-up "go/no go" decision-making journey paved with excitement and insecurities. From one start-up junkie to another, I wish you all the joy, pride, success and elation that your business adventure can offer.

Description

Designed for Business Students, Trainers, Fledging Entrepreneurs, and Tire Kickers

As start-up junkies, we are a unique tribe—inquisitive, keen, motivated, inspired, committed to succeed, and we have a profound love of business. Are you part of the tribe? Let's find out.

Business start-up advice needs to come from someone who has the bruises and laurels to prove that they have "skin in the game." Anything less is like getting child-rearing advice from your childless (but well-intentioned) Aunt Frieda.

In 30 steps, *The Start-Up Junkie's Playbook* leads you through a planning and introspective journey. It offers a unique viewpoint on getting into business, or when to walk away from your entrepreneurial dream—**the "go/no go" decision-making junction.**

The Start-Up Junkie's Playbook goes far beyond Business Plan thinking. Along with time-honored strategies, it also offers up a personal perspective for the fledgling entrepreneur, scrutiny of your interests and abilities, taking "pregnant pauses" to reflect and possibly tweak your business vision, questioning motives, and moving forward at your own pace.

Along the way, there are stories (often outrageous) about the author's experiences and those of his clients, as well as structured Workbooks accompanying each chapter to best understand and absorb what mentoring/counsel is being offered.

Keywords

entrepreneurial spirit; entrepreneurial mindset; entrepreneurial skills; entrepreneurial leadership; entrepreneurial advice; entrepreneurial advantages; entrepreneurial advantages and disadvantages; entrepreneurial decision making; steps for successful entrepreneurs; entrepreneurs playbook; entrepreneurs workbook; researching competition; small business growth; steps for successful small businesses; steps for start-ups;

writing successful business plans; family support in small businesses; entrepreneurship mindset; small business playbook; small business workbook; advice for small businesses; start-up success stories; start-up failure stories; quick tips for small business; quick tips for entrepreneurs; launching a small business

Contents

Testimonial

"I like the definitive nature and down to earth approach of this book—a clearly laid out roadmap that shows how to 'get it done' presented in a 'bam, bam' action-oriented format!

Having lived through several successful start-ups, I believe that 'Thirty Steps' provides entrepreneurs with a real foundation for reaching their goals."
—**Bruce E. McLean, Business Author**

Introduction

Introduction I: Business Starts Here

Planning a business needs to start somewhere. This Playbook can be it.

The objective of this manageable and plainspoken Playbook (and Workbook) is to sometimes gently, and sometimes less so, prod you toward making an informed decision about your proposed entrepreneurial undertaking or, conversely, by helping you realize and understand why you need to let go, walk away, and look elsewhere for opportunities.

That's the "go/no go" crossroads, likely the most important business decision you will ever have to make.

Think of this as a race to the starting line.

Get ready to walk through 30 consecutive tough and sometimes personal (even mildly cringe-worthy) step-by-step milestones packaged into the following:

- *Highlights*—Fully describe each step and how it fits into the overall entrepreneurial journey. Understanding the process is key.
- *Hurdles*—You will for sure encounter these. Everyone does. This section identifies the potential hurdles, including some off-beat uncommon roadblocks, and offers up realistic, doable mitigating strategies to traverse any piranha-infested streams.
- *Stories From the Trenches*—This section focuses on my "pleasure and pain" personal experiences, and not shying away from some pitfalls experienced by the start-up junkie author (i.e., me) and my clients and associates. Learning from others is wisdom steeped in the real world.
- *Action Planning/Workbook* —A Workbook follows each chapter, presented as progressive "baby steps" offered up in a commonsensical style and including how the expected

outcomes will likely impact that ambitious "empire-building" scenario dancing in your mind.

- *Appendix 1*—Located at the back of this book, this is a brief "*Glossary of Terms*" for business concepts that crop up in this Playbook and Workbook.
- *Appendix 2*—Contains a *Location Selection Guide and Checklist*, should the locale for your business be a consideration.

The Playbook and integrated Workbook will certainly increase your confidence and your abilities to deliver results and/or possibly save you from costly miscues and overzealous short-sighted leaps. Either way, you win.

Simply put, do the work. I know it sounds like a motherly scolding, but that is the absolute best way to maximize the mentoring benefits you will mine from this book.

Question: What sandbox do you play in?

- **Product or service business?** This Playbook and Workbook is for you.
- **Academia?** This book is an excellent resource for teachers, mentors, and trainers and an ideal accompaniment for entrepreneurship courses and workshops.
- **Consultant? Advisor?** Provides your business clients with a real-world perspective on entrepreneurship.

There is a certain wisdom that comes with age and business experience. I have been blessed with both and I am eager to share my entrepreneurial advice and stories with you. I like to think of this as communal therapy.

I have often been asked about *timelines. How long should this 30-step process take?* Every business is different in terms of size, complexity and planning, and funding requirements. However, generally speaking, look at a 90- to 120-day turnaround. Don't let your idea get stale-dated or obsolete. Incidentally, how many times have you heard someone expound on their idea and then add, "I have been working on this for years." They are dreamers, not entrepreneurs.

This Playbook will fit well with the author's existing three book collection with Business Expert Press, New York. www.businessexpertpress
.com/jay-j-silverberg/

1. *A Cynic's Business Wisdom: Winning Through Flexible Ethics* (2021)
2. *Dead Fish Don't Swim Upstream: Real Life Lessons in Entrepreneurship* (2022, coauthored with Bruce McLean)
3. *Stuck Entrepreneurs: Escape Routes Out of the Quicksand* (2023)

Introduction II: Ski Bikes—Committing Business Hari-Kari

There is joy in just the act of planning to launch a business. Part of that is a process of enduring a "proof of concept" where the idea is floated through various "prove it to me" stages, impartial research, trusted sounding board input, and critical-path planning, all of which precede your "go/no go" decision.

It's a thought-provoking safety net process, except if you happen to be someone so blinded by your own perceived brilliance that you ignore every red flag waving madly in your face.

Meet the Ski Bike inventors and self-proclaimed entrepreneurs: Two of the Three Stooges, whose concept of a bike on skis racing down a ski hill, followed a breakneck path of "never ever do this in business."

The third Stooge, incidentally, was in traction for months following a disastrous ski bike test run. He was like the kid Mikey of the Quaker Oats Life Cereal "Let Mikey try it" commercial. He was the punch line.

He bowed out of the venture. Being accosted and threatened with divorce by his wife was an added incentive, as was the loss of his savings earned selling psychoactive drugs. So, the original idea of a Ski Bike venture was not far removed from his likely drug-altered sense of safety.

But none of this deterred the two remaining partners from shushing full speed down the slopes of mishap and business failure. They were legends in their own cluttered minds. Their story is worth sharing.

The two lingering founders called upon me to help them find investors. I declined, but their story was like an accident in the making. I could not look away, so I followed the unfolding of their disaster as a captivated spectator.

Apparently, the Ski Bike was invented during a weekend up at the ski lodge. It was a simple contraption: skis mounted front and back over the bike's wheels, and added gripping plates installed as brakes to dig into the snow. Ice on the slopes diminished the braking capabilities, but this notion was beyond their ability to focus down on the small but critical details.

The one factor they forgot to entertain was that you really needed to be drunk or pharma-spaced to operate the Ski Bike because, when you fell, or were thrown off, which was a very likely scenario, a limber body bounced better.

They secured a patent, thinking there would be hordes of potential design infringements when reality proved the exact opposite. They had 100 percent of the market, whatever that was.

They produced a promotional video, carefully editing out the troubling falls and screams of panic of the on-screen riders. Elastic ethics, right?

They then succeeded in finding an investor, the owner of an idle bicycle factory in China, capable of producing the Ski Bikes.

The first batch of Ski Bikes was set up as rentals at a local ski resort. While the founders were astute enough to have riders sign waivers, there was no waiver strong enough to protect them from reckless negligence.

The very first weekend at the resort saw the busiest several days for the Ski Patrol, as most Ski Bike users were rescued and carted away in various states of personal disrepair.

It was all downhill from there.

Before "Ski Bikes 2" could be introduced, the lawsuits threatening the business mounted. The Chinese investor turned off the cash flow taps and the business collapsed, just like their Ski Bikes.

No market research, no real product testing, no product safety engineering, no feasibility, no risk analysis, no budgeting: a business idea built on naiveté, brashness, and endorphins.

Several months ago, I actually saw an ad selling a used Ski Bike. "Used only once" it said, and that spoke volumes.

Introduction III: Inspired Craziness

Anyone who has ever thought of going into business knows what a euphoric, almost orgasmic experience it can be—a sensory and emotional deluge.

I am a start-up junkie. Always have been. I proudly admit it. I am often the chaser of the shiny coins on the road, but experience has also taught me to distil my enthusiasm with a dollop of reality.

Having been on the entrepreneurial pathway on a hefty handful of occasions, I can tell you that the journey never gets old. It's new every time you take the leap, from the very first step onwards.

You are enraptured. Everything else in your life suddenly feels, well, different. Better. New.

Your concentration drifts away from the mundane of day-to-day, to visions of "wow" and "why not?"

The anticipation. The sleepless nights as images and ideas street-race through your imagination.

Single-mindedness overshadows all else. Everything related to your business vision takes on an urgent intensity.

Conversations about anything other than your business plans become relegated to small talk.

Even physical pains seem to become more manageable. Inconveniences. Business is the curative. I recall working on a pressing PowerPoint that I needed for a pending investor pitch, while ignoring an impacted tooth that cried for immediate root canal. Priorities, right?

Other worries diminish in urgency and importance. You know they will be dealt with once your business journey reaches its destination—success, as defined by your personal version of attainment.

Those disparaging frowns from your boss are not cringe-worthy anymore. Work becomes a holding bay while you dream and scheme.

If all of this sounds like an obsession, it is. Fixation on a singular stream of consciousness becomes your new addictive passion. Don't worry. It's all good. It all becomes a game.

Change is pending.

Even the uncertainty of it all gradually becomes more tolerable as concerns and challenges are conquered or slotted into categories of lesser importance. The harrowing "what if" mindset that can prevail with early-stage business explorers is silenced. You accept that it's all part of the cost of winning.

Entrepreneurship can be likened to a raucous, supercharged love affair between strangers, especially as you explore every nook and cranny that the opportunity offers and uncover all the dangers that a tryst can embody.

I now realize that I have made several sensual innuendos about the entrepreneurial journey. Rightly so, I suppose. Planning and starting a business is analogous to falling in love, or, at the very least, taking a lustful tumble.

And as in life, the process has its moments of stress, apprehension, and debilitating hindsight, all of which are part of building a relationship or, in fact, the act of birthing a business. These evil doers remind us that starting or growing a business can be likened to tiptoeing along a trail cluttered with gnarly exposed roots and hidden sinkholes, many of which can be avoided with the proper map.

Today, I am your travel guide, your business mentor.

The end goal we will achieve together is the beginning, namely, the "go/no go" decision making crossroads.

Your decision to proceed with your business initiative is the foundation upon which you can move forward and build. Conversely, if the outcome of this exercise is to discard your business scheme, then you can do so knowing that you have scrutinized and digested all aspects of the opportunity and found it lacking.

This "go/no go" junction is likely one of the most important intersections in the business planning crusade.

Let's simplify the journey. Getting to that critical "go/no go" crossroads can be accomplished by following 30 consecutive steps. It has worked for me and innumerable clients as well.

Remember that you are trying to decide whether you want to commit time, resources, focus, and your immediate future toward your entrepreneurial vision, so you had better be comfortable with your direction—not based on any knee-jerk decision, but one that is grounded on weighing all the facets of your intended venture and accepting the risks as much as you drool over the prospective rewards.

As you proceed, you may well discover that the business you will eventually be pursuing is not the model you started with. Things change. Plans and ideas morph. New facts and findings reveal themselves. Thoughts resolidify. And that's yet another benefit of following through the 30 steps that encourage you to think and reflect, and validate yet again.

Think of this voyage as the "Viagra trip." Remember that Viagra was invented as a blood pressure/hypertension med? As I said, things change along the way.

The pathway is a rambling one, with many alleyways that can entice you to veer off. *Try not to get distracted from your objectives. And try not to back-burner the process of getting you there either. Long respites cool enthusiasm.*

All possible outcomes from ecstatic to devastating need to be weighed and considered. The 30-Step Start-Up Junkie's Playbook (and Workbook) will help you understand and appreciate the process and provide you with the critical milestones for moving forward, or not.

Pay attention to the results.

Introduction IV: The Start-Up Junkie's 30-Step Journey

1. ***Dreaming and Scheming***: How ideas are born, and how each step of the "hatching" process provides the impetus to battle through all the inertia and hiccoughs that may follow suit. (And, yes, they usually do. Expecting them is a healthy attitude.)

2. ***The Frenetic Scribble***: The excitement of committing your roughed-out idea quickly to written or digital record. There is an urgency to just capture the moment.

3. ***Fleshing It Out***: As your riveting idea starts to germinate, you need to give it some body, giving some practical early thought to the actual Business Model. How will the business work? Starting a "pros and cons" list that gives equal consideration to both is critical, as is carrying out some frantic initial market research on steroids. The urgency is there.

4. ***Your First Sounding Board*** (please, not your mother): Packaging and presenting the idea to a trusted arms-length third party (while usually muttering the words "Am I crazy?" or "What am I missing here?"). Your expectations run high.

5. ***The Feedback Fallacy***: Learning to trust and fight the urge to ignore unappreciated feedback sometimes called "constructive criticism." Criticism can be perceived as deconstructive, even when it is constructive. It's human nature to resist any feedback other than "this is brilliant." Try harder. Keep an open mind.

6. ***Mindset and Commitment***: Wrapping your mind around the possibility of actually moving forward. It's a frame of mind the instant your attitude adopts an "I can do this" rationale. But at this point, you have likely not quite bought into this business 100 percent. There's more to be done, and you know it. Brace yourself. You have only completed 20 percent of the 30-step process.

7. ***Why Is Nobody Else Doing This?***: Trying to understand your niche and how you propose to stand out in the market. There is an insecurity working on you here. What don't you know?

8. ***Help Me Mr. Google***: Carrying out intensive web search and learning to filter out the nonsense or outdated stuff. Dealing with the valuable and valueless facts and fancy that web research regurgitates.

9. *Understand Your Competitors*: Carrying out competitive research, role modeling, and even interviewing similar companies outside your geographic targets, learning from others' successes and failures. This will test your communication and trust-building skills.

10. *Trend or Fad?*: Assessing if your business idea has "legs," and if it can stand the test of time. I once spent three months talking an entrepreneur down from starting a chain of vape shops. One year later, he sent me a generous thank you gift, which he stated represented about 5 percent of the investment he would have lost had he gone ahead with his idea. He jokingly also included a vape pen from a recently defunct vape chain.

11. *Who Will Buy This/Use This?*: An exercise in profiling, identifying your specific target market and audience. Your target market isn't the entire universe. Your decision to proceed with your business idea had better be more realistic. Zero in on your prospective customers/ clients.

12. *The Deep Dive Into Competition Research*: Coming down from the exhilaration of the 50,000-foot view, keep diving deep to explore who exactly you are up against, what they are doing that you should (or shouldn't) be copying, how you stack up to other players, and how best to compete in a competitive environment. All business environments are generally fiercely competitive. Count on it. Prepare for it.

13. *Growth Strategies*: There are a number of strategies the start-up entrepreneur should adopt right from the get-go. These will provide the framework for making decisions, dealing with changing markets, and fine-tuning people skills and other abilities that can become part of your successful growth arsenal. It's never too early to learn how to do things right.

14. *The Joys of Branding*: Beyond just a logo, how will you identify yourself to others, become recognizable and memorable? Branding is likely the most fun you will have in your business-building journey. It's amazing to see the image of your business come to life.

15. *Capture Customers*: How to capture a piece of the market even in a competitive, cutthroat marketplace. You will only get what you take, so develop a battle plan. Don't be so "nice."

16. ***Numbers Crunching: Fun With Figures***: Creative forecasting with real assumptions (no rose-colored glasses) and accepting that the reality of forecasted results rules your "go/no go" decision making and the ability to seek out funding.

17. ***Start-Up Needs***: Assessing what you need in terms of funding to launch, and what wealth and assets you personally bring to the table. Remember to add in six months of living on a peasant's income. Plan for worst case and enjoy anything beyond that.

18. ***Pause for a Checkup Report***: A self-administered checkup report. This is a "pregnant pause" that allows you to determine how far you have come in the 30-step Playbook Action Planning/Workbook tasks and what key steps still need to be carried out. Reflect. Second-guessing yourself, within reason, is fine, but do so constructively, not destructively.

19. ***Regulatory, Legalities, and Licensing***: The boring but necessary stuff and how to tackle it all without getting overwhelmed, jaded, or turned off. Get it done and move past it.

20. ***A Very Personal Perspective***: Taking measure from a personal vantage point. Are you the right person with the right skills and personality for this business? Will you get bored? Burnt out? Reckless? Distracted? Or, will you wonder what took you so long to take the leap?

21. ***Future Forward***: Are you comfortable seeing yourself in your chosen role down the road? Will this satisfy your entrepreneurial cravings?

22. ***Risk: Harnessing the Beast***: Quantifying the risk factors and whether or not you can limit or control them, and/or live with the exposure? If you feel your business opportunity has no risks, or very few, think again. If crossing the road or getting on a plane has inherent risks, imagine jumping into a situation that has 100+ variables, and "what-ifs," many of which should not be glossed over.

23. ***The Family as a Support Mechanism***: Family and friends are the groups most impacted by an entrepreneur's ultra-narrow focus on their business venture. Entrepreneurship is the newborn that squawks for attention. How will this venture impact your personal life, and will it be okay?

24. ***Money, Money, Money***: Every venture needs money. How much do you need and where will it come from? What can you offer up to get it? Learning to semigrovel for investment while on your Gucci kneepads is a useful business skill.

25. ***Your Business Model***: The critical pause button: taking a step back and a deep breath and looking at the overall business. How will your company operate and profit? Does it still make sense to you? Have you overthought? Underthought? Or Goldilocks' "just right" thinking?

26. ***Your Value Proposition***: Let's make sure that your products or services create value for your customers. It had better do so, or customers will go elsewhere. Customers tend to be fickle.

27. ***Your Business Plan Like No Other***: Finally, this is the brain dump, putting everything you have learned into a presentation written for yourself personally, as well as for a target readership: You? Investors? Potential partners? Funders? Each reader expects something a little different in terms of content and style. So, figure it out before you expend an ounce of effort.

28. ***You and Your Devil's Advocate***: Exactly what it sounds like, carrying out a serious re-examination of your proposed business venture and your ability and willingness to run it. Plan for contingencies and a Plan B. Find someone to play "devils' advocate" and pay attention to their probing questions. Prepare yourself mentally for the demands of entrepreneurship. Getting your personal, financial, and professional houses in order before you launch.

29. ***More Tales and Lessons From the Trenches***: Every business experience has a story, and every story provides a lesson. Good or bad, comforting or heartbreaking, funny or sad, experience teaches us that business is just human.

30. ***Go/No Go?***: One more decision. You have reached the "go/no go" crossroads. Based on all the above, is this business ready to launch, or not? Before you press the start button, there are a number of *entrepreneurial truisms* that you need to understand. These truisms I am sharing are derived from my own business life experiences. I am certain that they will add a real-world perspective to your "go/no go" decision making.

Appendixes

Appendix 1: Glossary of Business Terms is a compendium of terms used throughout this book and their definitions.

Appendix 2: Location Selection Guide and Checklist is a useful planning tool, should the local of your business be an important consideration.

Here is the 30-step start-up business junkie's journey, in a simplified format.

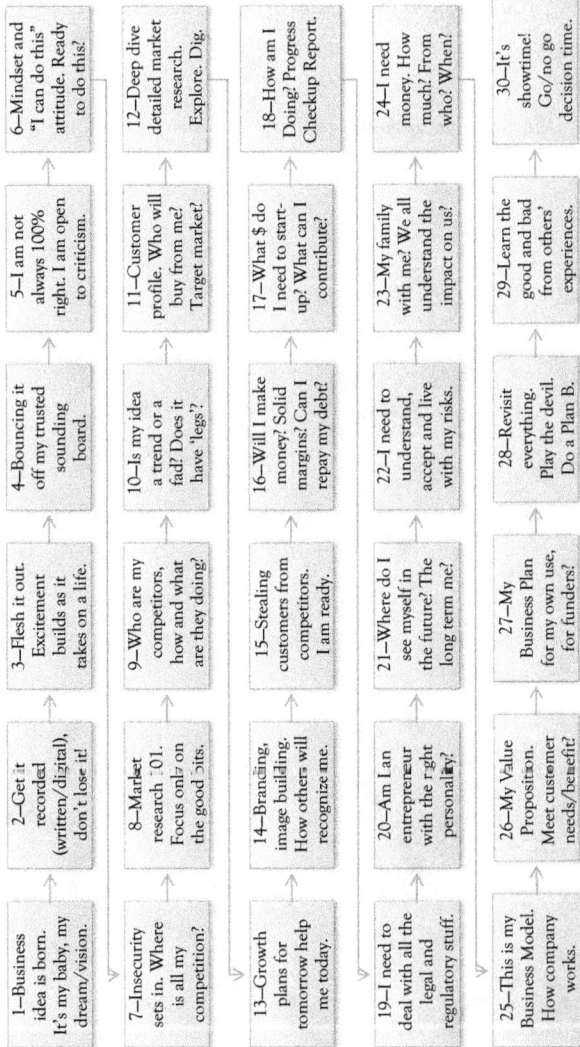

1–Business idea is born. It's my baby, my dream/vision.

2–Get it recorded (written/digital), don't lose it!

3–Flesh it out. Excitement builds as it takes on a life.

4–Bouncing it off my trusted sounding board.

5–I am not always 100% right. I am open to criticism.

6–Mindset and "I can do this" attitude. Ready to do this?

7–Insecurity sets in. Where is all my competition?

8–Market research 101. Focus only on the good bits.

9–Who are my competitors, how and what are they doing?

10–Is my idea a trend or a fad? Does it have 'legs'?

11–Customer profile. Who will buy from me? Target market?

12–Deep dive detailed market research. Explore. Dig.

13–Growth plans for tomorrow help me today.

14–Branding, image building. How others will recognize me.

15–Stealing customers from competitors. I am ready.

16–Will I make money? Solid margins? Can I repay my debt?

17–What $ do I need to start-up? What can I contribute?

18–How am I Doing? Progress Checkup Report.

19–I need to deal with all the legal and regulatory stuff.

20–Am I an entrepreneur with the right personality?

21–Where do I see myself in the future? The long term me?

22–I need to understand, accept and live with my risks.

23–My family with me? We all understand the impact on us?

24–I need money. How much? From who? When?

25–This is my Business Model. How company works.

26–My Value Proposition. Meet customer needs/benefit?

27–My Business Plan for my own use, for funders?

28–Revisit everything. Play the devil. Do a Plan B.

29–Learn the good and bad from others' experiences.

30–It's showtime! Go/no go decision time.

CHAPTER 1

Dreaming and Scheming

Highlights

Ideas for your business sometimes come from the oddest of inspirations. They attack your imagination and imbed themselves into your daytime and nighttime dreams. They own you.

But here's the thing: The harder you consciously struggle to actively think of an opportunity as you sit in front of your laptop, fingers impatiently Ouija-boarding across your keyboard, the likelier that the idea will be a "dog"—unreachably high, dreary, or a demoralizingly also-ran. Don't be discouraged.

Entrepreneurs tend to be free thinkers. Independent-minded. Unless you are someone who would actually enjoy going on vacation with your aging in-laws on a painfully organized senior's bus tour to visit every lawnmower museum in the country, you need to appreciate that business ideas and opportunities arrive impromptu. They waltz in and create an "aha" moment. But what are the opportunity launching pads?

The most conventional ones tend to follow one of these patterns:

- From work experience. This is an obvious one. You want to be your own boss in a business you already know something about. There is a comfort level there.
- An idea you picked up at a trade show where you encountered a thousand other nomads wandering the halls in search of a business opportunity. The competition can be off-putting, especially when you approach an exhibitor and hear "Funny you mentioned that. There have been 25 other inquiries…."
- Converting a hobby or craft. The danger here is that the joy derived from your pastime becomes a burden when you must do it for a living.

- Copycats. While there is nothing wrong with replicating existing businesses, the more diehard start-up junkie will get bored with this approach. It can be successful but yet unfulfilling.
- Something you read about on social media or some boastful Internet site, like "Worm Farmers Make Millions." There is always an inherent danger in believing false prophets.

Now let's have a look at a few more creative sources of business opportunities:

- Network. Become an idea magnet at every personal encounter, both business and pleasure. Stimulate conversation whenever you can. It is quite amazing how ideas bubble up at these get-togethers. Learn to listen.
- Join a company and learn everything you can. Move through the hierarchy of career positions. You will know when you are ready to leave the nest.
- Symbiosis, or rather "mutualism": develop a mutually beneficial relationship; that is where both parties benefit. In layman's jargon, that's building a "win–win" situation where they need you and you use them to fulfill what you need, such as an existing distribution channel or an existing brand you can market under. Let's call it a "use–use."
- Look for market gaps. Every marketplace has fissures that can represent a need you can fill.
- Vertical integration is an interesting avenue to explore. There are existing products or services that could benefit from moving up their value-adding chain, stuff the companies may be aware of but don't have the time or ability to act on. That's where you come to the rescue. You coattail on others, making it easier for you to penetrate sought-after markets. Again, it's "use–use," which is actually a de facto business strategy.
- Ideas also come from need. If you can't find a job or are burnt out in your current career, you will find that ideas

and opportunities have an enhanced playing field in your mind. Just don't jump out of anger or desperation. Either one can color your logic.

Hurdles

The most predominant hurdles you may encounter are fact based: tough market penetration, unattractive returns, competition, launch or operating funds shortage, and all the components of diligent opportunity planning and research. However, the greatest roadblock you may encounter is not quantifiable. It's your mindset, your way of thinking.

The biggest hurdle that I have encountered, both for myself and for my clients, was mind games. That translates to lack of confidence in your ability to make the right decision, or any decision, for that matter. Cold feet. Night sweats. Second (and third and fourth) thoughts. Call it what you will, it manifests itself into entrepreneurial immobility.

Part of the opportunity analysis you should carry out is taking a personal inventory of your willingness and interests in launching a business that will likely become your shadow for the foreseeable future. Is this what you want? Do you like the role, time, and focus it will demand of you?

This is the soft side of business, the stuff that does not lend itself to spreadsheets and market analysis. Your decision to proceed or walk away is impacted by your core values and gut feel, and it is every bit as important.

It's your basic "fear or flight" reflex. It swirls unabatedly in your mind, often battling, or, at best, auditing your reasoning. It tempers your excitement. It is telling.

Pay attention. It is your safety valve.

Tales From the Trenches

In my youth, I contemplated a career in photography. I enjoyed camerawork and darkroom as a hobby until I landed a job cranking out newborn baby pictures for a photography service. (I tell people that I used to make about 50 babies a week. That's always been a conversational icebreaker.)

After I quit, I didn't touch my camera again for a few years because all I ever saw through my viewfinder was an image of toothless, bubbling smiles of a cacophony of two-day-old droolers. Sometimes personal experience does you no favors.

I knew a stock day-trader who blogged advice on investment and flaunted his successes. After he surprisingly declared personal bankruptcy, I asked him how it was possible, seeing that he never lost a penny. Elastic ethics. Don't take anything people say at face value. People lie. Dig deeper.

In one particular case, I was presented with an opportunity to be part of a public offering. The payback was impressive. The risks, as explained to me, were controllable (always are, right?!). Yet, there was something about the players that tweaked my early warning system. Could they be trusted, and did I want to be associated with them? It was a struggle between greed and nagging disquietude. I chose to walk away and watched from the sidelines as they subsequently went down in flames. Listen to your inner voice. It's like your mother scolding you to "stop that." It rarely lets you down.

Action Planning/Workbook

1. At this stage, carry out preresearch, prefeasibility analysis, and risk analysis, all of which are covered in subsequent steps in this playbook/ workbook. It's time to dream and scheme.
2. Make a list of the five things that interest you as far as possibly building a business around. Do not include stuff like "emulate Elon Musk" or anything that might not be a realistic reach (or a questionable role model?).
3. For each of those, list five reasons why you feel you can and will succeed.
4. List out what you bring to the table in terms of experience, assets, and connections to facilitate launching and/or running the business.
5. Now, it's time to get personal. How do feel, personally, about involving yourself in this prospective venture? Can you see yourself being responsible for everything and everyone…every day?

6. As you begin to narrow down your favorite possibilities, list who you must "bring to the table" to get this initiative launched. The expression "lowest hanging fruit" is key. The more outside parties, investors, strategic partners, government regulatory agencies, and the like, the longer and tougher it gets. There is the danger of running out of steam, better defined as losing interest, before you open your doors.

7. By now, you will have narrowed your focus, and it is time to move on to the next step. Congratulations. You have framed your business foundation. Rest up for the next 29 steps.

CHAPTER 2

The Frenetic Scribble

Highlights

Other than falling deeply in love (romantic, lustful, or otherwise), the birth of your much anticipated first born, or winning the mega lottery, the majesty and mind-numbing impact of the business idea "aha moment" has no rival.

It arrives with a thud and simply won't go away. It worms itself into your conscience and pops up to the forefront of your thoughts at the weirdest and sometimes most inappropriate of times.

The frenetic scribble deserves some form of immortality.

Learn that your phone's voice recorder is your friend. Before the advent of cellphones, when dinosaurs roamed the earth, I always kept a pad of paper and a pen close by. Not the most effective means of recording your thoughts when you are driving, or in the shower, or at 3 a.m. awoken by a fleeting brainstorm. I learned to perfect the art of writing in the dark and the ability to decipher the hieroglyphics of my nocturnal transcripts.

Every thought is brilliant at the time of its birth, but it is an ongoing process. Business opportunities have an ebb-and-flow character to them. Delays have a price. They change, take on new directions, or even implode when the idea's realizability gets questioned or quashed by reason or doubt. Or lack of available funds.

Regardless, the entire process demands the diligent journalizing of ideas and thoughts, even rambling ones, and in whatever form you will steadfastly maintain.

Keep a journal or a giant whiteboard. I have always felt that it needs to be something visual. I would sit for hours staring at my whiteboard scribbles hoping for some breakthrough firebolt to fill whatever gaps that were obstructing my business vision. I still do it. It is almost a meditative process. My mantra is "what if I try changing this?"

Hurdles

Things change, and you need to keep up with it. The danger is that entrepreneurs tend to be leery to drift away from anything other than their original ideas. Any variations can cause consternation. It's like you are on a forced march, but with blinders. Does that sound familiar?

The key is to stay open to an inevitable change of direction while you maintain your high level of entrepreneurial enthusiasm. Tough tag team, but necessary.

And remember one of the cardinal rules of validating your business; the business you are planning today may not be the venture you end up launching. Stay attuned to shifting boundaries.

Tales From the Trenches

A restaurant napkin served as the scribble notepad for one of my most successful business brainchildren (plural of brainchild?). My idea was scrawled under the restaurant's imprinted napkin tag message: *We're small, but we think BIG!* Karma, right? I kept the napkin framed over my desk as a constant reminder of inspired craziness.

Using a voice recorder, tablet, cellphone, or other gadget to document your thoughts is a useful practice, except when you find yourself in a restaurant washroom, in midstream, and incapable of letting go of an idea.

It happened to me. I quickly snuck into a stall and frantically dictated all my thoughts into my phone in fear of losing any miniscule fragment of my "brilliance." When I emerged, sweaty and fulfilled, there was a security guard waiting to greet me. He did not share my exuberance. It didn't matter. My thoughts were now enshrined.

Action Planning/Workbook

1. Try various methods of tracking the progress of your idea as it evolves—notes on your phone or laptop, journal, recorder, whiteboard, flowchart, or any technique that allows you to look back at your progress to learn from your past labors.
2. Make them visual on a poster or computer home screen.

3. Take your idea for a walk. Literally! This is an effective method to clear your mind and create an open environment for you to work on your thoughts. I have always used forest trails or quiet beachfront.

4. Set up a weekly schedule to review the status that all started with your frenetic scribble.

CHAPTER 3

Fleshing It Out

Highlights

"You're too skinny. You need to eat more, take better care of yourself." My mother's favorite admonishments as she led me down the road to childhood corpulence. Fleshing out your business idea(s) is no different.

You know your business idea is a great one. A can't-lose proposition. Of course you feel that way. Your endorphins are streaming through you. Your imagination is firing and filling you with dreams of humongous returns, infamy, and visions of fulfillment. Now what?

Conjuring up a business opportunity is not a fact-based process. It is the stuff that sugarplum faeries dole out. All the sweet, and very little substance. It is all good, but not good enough to carry you beyond the jumping off point. It is the springboard on which you hang your hopes.

Once the preliminary one-person celebrations begin to wane, a modest sense of foreboding begins to settle in. "How will this business actually work? Can I do it? This is going to be a lot of work. Do I even want to do it? Can I afford it? Seriously, can I pull this off?" I can already hear the whispers of doubt. The tasks feel daunting, but they are not.

You have undoubtedly done some very preliminary research and found nothing wanting in your idea, which is highly typical of early-stage dreaming and scheming. Everything is wonderful and one of your greatest fears is that someone else will leapfrog you before you reach the starting line, or you have forgotten to figure something into the equation.

Paranoia is a mainstay of early-stage opportunity concept development. You clutch your idea close to you even more than you would protect your knapsack in a crowded Romanian market brimming with shadowy gypsy street urchins and pickpockets.

This sense of doubt is healthy. It is your safety valve kicking in, warning you that although you are undeniably a dazzling entrepreneur, and you just KNOW you are, there's something missing from the big picture—namely the big picture.

It's time to flesh out your idea, to give it more substance, detail, and fabric (interesting that we still use the literal phrase "fleshing it out" first cited in the 1600s to describe the act of putting meat on the bones of your business opportunity).

Why you do this is self-evident:

- To prove your idea will work
- To identify any gaps or flaws
- To gage the feasibility and viability of the idea
- To gain confidence in moving your plans forward
- Mostly, to begin to visualize your Business Model

However, there's more to it insofar as you need to consider who your audience will be:

- There is a need to be realistic once your idea takes hold and you begin to fill in the blanks of how it will actually work.
- If the ultimate audience is funders, government granting agencies, investors, and/or prospective partners, you absolutely need to research and understand what drives each of them. What are the hot buttons that influence their decision making? Your "fleshing out" process needs to be keenly aware of the other party's motivation in possibly dealing with you.
- Investors' rally cry is often "PPE," that being "profits, protection of investment, and exit strategies." Long-term potential is keynote. Every funder is searching for an "Elon Muskless Elon Musk" (enough is enough, right?). Downstream potential payback is a huge factor.
- For traditional funders, the important factors are security, ability to reimburse their investment, and your character, including your creditworthiness.

- For government grants/funders, each agency has their "raison d'etre," that is, why they do what they do. Do your homework. Check them out before submitting anything. Their websites will tell you everything you need to know.

When you undertake this fleshing out process of making your plan more substantial, it's important to focus on what your issues, opportunities, and risks are, as well as the factors that drive other parties whom you wish to attract and embrace in the process.

Once again, it is important that, at this stage, your role is to expand on your business opportunity, keeping in mind that there are still 27 steps in your journey before you arrive at an unequivocal "go/no go" decision.

Hurdles

The greatest challenges in the fleshing out process are (1) impartiality and (2) honesty.

At some point, you will need to adopt a bit of a spectator vantage point where you can see clearly, that is, recognize both the good and bad in your idea(s).

Honesty is the ability to accept your preliminary results without coloring what you find to fit your vision of the opportunity. You cannot always be your own cheerleader.

Tales From the Trenches

One of my initiatives was to capture the jade supply market in western Washington, British Columbia, and Alaska. Jade is a valuable commodity in China, and there is great demand, as exemplified by hordes of black marketeers arriving from Asia with bags of money. Literally, plastic grocery bags brimming with cash.

I had the connections in place to corner the jade supply chain and was told repeatedly that the industry worked on handshake deals. I shook a lot of hands. I was on a "couldn't fail" course.

I fleshed out my all-too-brief Business Model based on assumptions made on promises and greed—suppliers' promises and my blinding greed.

Just before the first big shipment, my suppliers called for a meeting at which they introduced an unexpected interloper, Mr. Yan. He proceeded to show me a tattered designer suitcase (likely a fake) stuffed with money. He laughingly toyed with his own white jade necklace and boasted it was worth more than my house. The suppliers' allegiance to me vanished.

Fleshing out your Business Model means trying to make it foolproof, and not being foolhardy. Don't make knee-jerk presumptions. There are lots of Mr. Yans who can end run your business dream.

Action Planning/Workbook

1. Give some practical early thought to the actual Business Model. How will the business work?
2. Starting a "pros and cons" list that gives equal consideration to both is critical, as is carrying out some frantic initial market research on steroids.
3. Flip the coin over. Think of five things that can negatively impact the business. What are they and how can they be avoided or dealt with?
4. Create a one to two pager outlining your proposed venture, fleshed out, and include the following:
   a. Why you think it will succeed.
   b. Why you feel there is a market or need.
   c. A very simple overview of the Business Model, without giving the secrets away.
   d. Why you are the best person to launch and run it.
   e. What can stop you in your tracks.
5. Get ready to seek some sounding board input as described in the next step. Rehearse. Get comfortable pitching the idea.

CHAPTER 4

Your First Sounding Board

Highlights

While your business idea is still barely a fetus, the use of a sounding board is a great way to gain an independent, third-party take on what has been dominating your every thought.

It is you delivering a brain dump to a select and respected listener, preferably someone with a business or entrepreneurial background. Caution must be exercised in not choosing someone who may deliver skewed advice, and that includes close friends who may be jealous or your mom and dad who may still see you as the youngster sheepishly bringing home that first report card. Get some neutrality.

The business sounding board is likely the first person with whom you are sharing your idea(s), so there is a little apprehension in the process. You may choose to use a Non-Disclosure Agreement ("NDA"), but, frankly, they do not hold much weight in providing a safe forum. The NDA is psychological security, but if it gives you greater peace of mind, and they are willing to sign it, then it is an option worth considering.

Regardless, the sounding board experience is like a trip to the confessional: a sigh of relief after you unload. It is a therapeutic process.

I have always been a big believer in using sounding boards for numerous reasons. Sounding boards deliver **qualitative** and **quantitative** results.

Quantitative Deliverables	Qualitative Deliverables
Confirms that you are on the right track OR, conversely, allows you to shift your thinking to alternate avenues or changes to your opportunity planning	Open discussion frees your mind to expand your perspective of your business opportunity
Provides a new perspective from a different vantage point	Builds your entrepreneurial confidence

(Continues)

(*Continued*)

Quantitative Deliverables	Qualitative Deliverables
Challenges your thinking in a nonthreatening environment	Relieves "mental constipation/overload." At some point in the process, your mind cannot process much more until you share the load with a sounding board
Stimulates your creativity and vision, including revisiting preliminary numbers, targets, and launch costs	Allows you to explore without any related dangers or repercussions
Can result in identifying benefits and risks you had not considered. An outside counsel may see things you do not see or do not want to see	Would likely deliver a reality check/grounding so vital in moving your idea forward
Helps you avoid costly mistakes and misappropriated start-up costs	Belays feeling of insecurity or confusion
Avoids time delays, stalling your launch, and missing any window of opportunity	Validates your feeling of excitement. All new entrepreneurs thrive on some positive reinforcement
Delivers direction for your initiative. This sounds simple, but when you are wearing blinders that do not permit peripheral vision, outside direction can offer up critical advice to keep you on course or to chart a slightly new order to your world	Just need to talk. Sometimes it's as simple as having someone to occasionally or regularly bounce around ideas, concerns, challenges, and direction. And sometimes it's just about "business companionship." Everyone needs a friend to talk to
Allows you to be challenged	Explaining your ideas to others can help you clarify your own thinking and provide direction that may be obscured, or lost amidst the multitude of thoughts rambling about in your mind
Avoids the temptation of acting on your own for the sake of moving forward faster	

Hurdles

Trust—This becomes an impeding issue if you seek out mentor/counsel from a third party you do not know well. Finding the right individual(s) is key.

Listen, or not listen—Go into it with an open mind, or don't go there at all.

Believing only what you want to believe—The cliché is about a person who has cancer and seeks out advice from his doctor who declares he has three months to live. Unhappy with this diagnosis, the patient sees out second, third, and fourth doctors' advice, all of whom give him three to five months to live. The sixth doctor declares the patient's cancer is likely in remission and not to worry so much. The patient returns home and exclaims to his partner "I am cured!"

Don't only believe what you want to hear.

Tales From the Trenches

I was approached by a bright young technology client who purported to have a game-changing idea (they are always market disrupters). Not having enough depth in this particular sector, I organized a question and answer session with a few guest investor-type friends to act as an independent sounding board.

They shot the entrepreneur's idea full of holes and seriously questioned its realizability, numbers, market share projections, and Business Model. They saw this as the equivalent of VHS in a world of digital downloads, which was pretty demeaning, albeit seemingly honest.

The techie claimed to have "proof of concept" and held firm. He then launched his business with family money. Apparently, his family, despite their limited tech market knowledge, considered the entrepreneur/son a "technology visionary." I must have heard them quote that a hundred times.

The business was launched to appeal to a small following that soon became a miniscule niche market. The demise followed within six months.

This is worth repeating: don't just listen to advice you want to hear, and ignore the biased kudos from your family

Action Planning/Workbook

1. Find someone(s) to act as your sounding board(s). Interview them. Make sure they have some knowledge of your type of business but no direct or indirect investment or ownership in any potential competitor.
2. Prepare your PowerPoint Deck that best exemplifies the best-selling features of your proposed opportunity.

3. Practice its delivery on a tablet or laptop. Either of these will be useful tools to deliver your message.

4. Prepare and practice an "elevator pitch" that can blend with your Deck.

5. Lay out rules for the sounding board as to what you expect from them.

   a. Ability to listen and question what they may not understand.

   b. Ask questions, even probing ones, that explore the opportunity, its risks, and claimed rewards.

   c. Verbalize issues and concerns in an honest manner.

   d. No interference with any personal agendas they may harbor.

   e. Deliver unfettered feedback, both good and bad.

CHAPTER 5

The Feedback Fallacy

Highlights

"Would you mind if I give you some feedback wrapped in the pretext of constructive criticism?"

Your jaw clenches shut, teeth grinding in the process. Your hands death-grip the chair armrests. Your body tenses as it prepares for the intrusion and the attack on your senses and sensitivities.

Constructive criticism is an oxymoron, in the same league as "progressive conservative," "awfully good," or "jumbo shrimp." It oozes contradiction.

It doesn't need to inflict pain. In fact, it should be a rewarding experience that identifies the strengths that others see in your fledgling business venture as well as generally creative solutions to issues, challenges, and gaping holes in your Business Model. That's all good.

The key for you, the recipient of any constructive criticism, is to focus on the positivity of the experience from comments and suggestions that can be acted on to improve your business opportunity. Anything less can be classified as destructive criticism, its evil twin.

Here are some defining moments in "feedback fallacy" and how to assure the process of constructive criticism is actually productive.

- Certainly, the onus on your part is to fight your natural instincts that make you defensive. Mental roadblocks to receiving feedback virtually negate the interaction.
- All parties need to look at constructive criticism as an appraisal of facts and not a judgment of the entrepreneur's performance.
- Pay more attention to what is working instead of what is not.

- There needs to be a certain harmony between the giver and the receiver. Both need to be open-minded and on a like course of conversation.
- Feedback is never 100 percent accurate or useful. Sort out the "good bits" that you can take away from the encounter.
- In some instances, those providing feedback inject their personal bias into the process instead of focusing on the business opportunity issues being reviewed. Cut off any dialog where the sender is expressing a personal prejudice. For example, "I don't believe in that" is not at all helpful. Ask why not?
- Constructive criticism works best if you are told what to do better as opposed to what you did wrong.

Hurdles

Don't take anything personally. It is human nature to feel that criticism about something you are doing reflects directly on who you are.

There is a need to separate the "business you" from the "personal you." Viewing anything that is said as a personal affront simply shuts down the process of useful interaction because it shuts off your ability or willingness to absorb anything.

You should not accept those dishing out advice/feedback to adopt the role of the parent in a parent–child relationship. Here's an example.

- I had a partner who would approach constructive criticism with me by saying, "I have something I need to talk to you about." I learned quickly that the phrase was the opening salvo whereby he would unload on me for stuff dredged from both the recent and distant past, like he maintained a cave of derision where he stored his barbed arrows.
- I learned to respond with the likes of "Not now. I will let you know when I am actually in the mood to be the dumpee." This proved to deflate the power of my partner.
- Overall, this did not bode well for our ill-fated partnership.

Tales From the Trenches

I had an interest in an air purification technology company that used ultra violet C to remove odors, organic compounds, and bacteria particles from the air. The target markets were commercial buildings, hospitals, cruise ships, and airplanes.

The technology worked well, as proven in controlled and extensive laboratory testing. The problem was that the results were invisible to prospective buyers. You could not sense or feel it working. All you saw was a big machine emitting a light, while fans whirred and circulated the air, like a giant Dr. Seuss "Throm-dim-bu-lator."

I needed to give our sales force a vital tool. I assembled a group of industry stakeholders and scientific academia players and presented our problem.

Over the course of our feedback sessions, I listened carefully to everything that was suggested. I received 10 potential solutions. Three were jokingly impractical. Four were quack suggestions with no possible way to implement. Three had some merit, the best of which was to develop a chemically sensitive demo pad that turned red in the presence of airborne contaminants and then cleared when the machine worked its magic.

Our marketing door-opener was born. Sales increased dramatically.

In year three, I sold my shares in the company. A typical start-up junkie exit strategy.

Action Planning/Workbook

1. Prepare an agenda of issues, opportunities, and challenges on which you would like feedback.
2. Practice listening to others. While this sounds simple, it is not an easy skill to perfect. Encourage friends and family to help you develop a thick skin and not take critiques personally. Toughen up your sensitive ego.
3. Select a group of receptive, third-party people whose opinion you respect.
4. Run the meet, set the pace, don't get immersed in any deconstructive dialog.

5. Agree to disagree on anything contentious; then take the time to revisit and decide a course of action.

6. Look for commonality. When you start hearing the same kind of advice or suggestions, pay attention. Useable feedback has been achieved.

CHAPTER 6

Mindset and Commitment

Highlights

Whether your glass is half empty or half full, the glass is refillable! It's your positive mindset and attitude that will fill it up.

It may sound like we are wandering into a "feel good/touchy feely" world populated by aging, brittle, paunchy hippie types (no, it does not describe me), but, in fact, this is the underrated, often overlooked soft belly of entrepreneurship that demands respect. Let's jump in.

Your *mindset* and *commitment* are the interconnected forces that give you the strength, mental attitude, and determination to push forward to reach a "go/no go" decision that you can live with. The key words here are "can live with," embracing the outcome that you will reach at the end of this 30-step exercise.

So, how do you prepare yourself?

Mindset	Commitment
Approach your goals with an open, accepting mind, not fixed by predetermined conclusions	Stay focused and jealously protect your priorities
Adopt an "abundance mindset" that allows and encourages you to seek and accept more ideas, including those offered up by others	If entrepreneurial passion is part of your commitment, you will not likely be impacted by any negativity that can and will swirl around you
Avoid being defensive as this limits your ability to listen and harvest advice	Committed businesspeople have goals which they perceive as attainable. Regardless, they are dreamers steadfast in their belief
When seeking input from others you have chosen to approach, assume that they are good at what they do and have something to offer you. They are worthy mentors	Goals may change but the level of commitment to your "flavor of the day" goal should not

(Continues)

(*Continued*)

Mindset	Commitment
Trust that you have the ability to filter what is doable/implementable or not	Committed people are happy because they have definable dreams and aspirations that they can see and feel
Understand that success is created. Don't take it for granted	Commitment is having the courage to trek into unknown territory
Sometimes, in moving forward, there are periods of standing still patiently, and/or taking a step back and reflecting on the big picture	Acceptable levels of risk can motivate you, but should not freeze your journey before you reach that critical "go/no go" crossroads. Commitment is the driver

Hurdles

One of the worst setbacks that can plague you is losing focus and allowing indecision and procrastination to dominate your ability to act. Stay in the here and now.

Time is one of your greatest commodities. Distraction eats time, expending it without any real purpose.

Falling into the pit of negative thought can set you back. Giving yourself reasons why you "can't" or "shouldn't" is counterproductive and dangerously wasteful.

Adopt this mantra *"I have had many problems in my life, and most of them have never happened."*

Understand that failure and setbacks are great teachers. If you are unwilling to learn, no one can help you.

Unfortunately, struggle is an ever-present nasty detractor of entrepreneurship. It can infiltrate your mindset and weaken your commitment. Knowing in advance that this can and will likely happen, will help you resist any temptation to backtrack on your business initiative.

Tales From the Trenches

One of my favorite personal achievement stories was my launching and spearheading the growth of a multinational consulting firm. Over five years, the firm grew to include a number of branch and associate offices across North America and an arsenal of bright (and extremely well-groomed and stylishly dressed) young consultants.

That's the jubilant conclusion to this business opportunity journey. Getting there was a grind.

My mindset was cast. I was determined to implement a Business Model that had undergone the scrutiny of several colleagues. Plus, my own planning and judicious due diligence supported my decision to proceed.

My commitment was based on necessity since I was restless after undergoing several career changes. I needed to find something exciting, and when nothing presented itself, entrepreneurship was the preferred fallback position.

Building market awareness and capturing a minutia of market share were challenging. The big firms wouldn't let me join the Boys Club. I had the skills, but struggled to gain a foothold.

My approach was built on "elastic ethics," harmlessly embellishing the truth about my company. Which one of us has never puffed up our websites and corporate profiles? I skated. Nothing stopped me.

I succeeded. My keenly focused mindset and unwavering commitment worked.

After five years, in typical start-up junkie fashion, I sold the company. It was (and is) my modus operandi.

The lesson here is that a focused, determined mindset, coupled with a strategic dose of creativity and an unshakeable commitment can be your foundation to fulfilling your business vision.

Action Planning/Workbook

1. List five positive and five negative features that best describe your mindset, that is, your "stick-to-it-ness" outlook when it comes to work, business, or a relationship.

2. Select three close associates and let them query the features you listed. How did you perform?

3. What strategies can you undertake to rid yourself of the identified negative mindsets?

4. List five events in your life where you showed great commitment to something. How did each end up?

5. Do you feel you have an "abundance mindset," that is, the ability to stay committed and motivated? If yes, explain. You need to convince only yourself.

6. List five goals you have in life. How committed are you to each, and why?

7. Assuming mindset and commitments are interrelated, can you explain to yourself how this joint relationship works to your advantage? What might you do to better integrate this duo into your makeup?

CHAPTER 7

Why Is Nobody Else Doing This?

Highlights

We entrepreneurs are insecure souls. We thrive on attention, nervously seeking hordes of adoring clients/customers and even groupies. It's almost cult-like. Being loved is our security blanket.

But we are also threatened when we hear the footsteps of competition encroaching on our turf—real or perceived threats, zeroing in on the bullseye targets on our backs.

All of that having been said, we feel most insecure standing out in a field of nothing and nobody. You find yourself in a dilemma fed by self-doubt. Where is everyone? Why are there no (or very few) other businesses playing in my sandbox? What am I doing wrong?

This solitude might be cause for quiet celebration, not whiny panic.

Your Business Model follows one of these pathways.

1. You are copycatting or coattailing an existing business, in which case you have little reason to be threatened about launching into a dark chasm.

2. You are doing something that hasn't been done before. You are a visionary with Steve Jobs and Mark Zuckerberg motivational posters adorning your office. Peter Thiel (Mr. billionaire PayPal) encourages entrepreneurs to "Solve a problem that nobody else is solving, and dominate that space." I like that.

3. There is little or no competition in the niche you have chosen. You may very well own 90 percent of a Lilliputian marketplace, or at least that's how you feel. Your insecurity has shifted into overdrive. Unless your margins are huge, a large share of a small market niche is worth you revisiting your Business Model.

4. Somebody had previously tried a similar business, and it didn't work. You are reasonably certain you can do it better, do it right. You can learn from predecessors' mistakes. There's your positive mindset talking!

5. Sometimes novelty is just novelty, a fad with a short lifespan. Nobody is doing it because nobody wants it.

If you are immersed in slightly numbing insecurity and self-doubt, you are not alone. A significant number of early-stage or would-be entrepreneurs quit in response to their fear-or-flight protective instinct.

Second-guessing and emotional decision making are fruitless exercises. Deal with the facts.

It is time to step back and affirm where your business idea came from, how it evolved, and, most importantly, why you feel people will buy it or use it. That is, "enough" people who can make your venture profitable and sustainable.

Hurdles

Every business has risks: personal, financial, technological, and, yes, even emotional. You need to set what risk factors you are comfortable living with and have your venture take place within those acceptable parameters.

Changes are inherent in business, particularly during the embryonic stage. However, too many entrepreneurs do not have a Plan "B" that can be implemented should Plan "A" become unlaunchable. It is wise for you to have a fallback position.

Risks and rewards are the cornerstones of business. Your idea(s) may be great, but the costs may outweigh any rewards. Or payback goes beyond your cash flow's ability to carry the load or repay debt. Don't let prospective rewards block out any shadows cast by risks.

Tales From the Trenches

Don't invent or develop products because you think they are kind of "cool," but without any idea as to who will buy them. I have witnessed this a multitude of times in the technology and health care fields:

$30,000 stereo speakers for the elite but small stereophile community; an ultra-effective medical software package for tracking patients that was, alas, incompatible with most hospital record-keeping systems (the cost of compatibility was prohibitive); right down to a toilet seat with built in Bluetooth and Wi-Fi, for when the user just couldn't wait.

The list is almost endless. The simple rule is "will your target audience enthusiastically be reaching for their credit cards?" They had better.

In China, there is a phenomenon called "swarming." Groups of people all interested in buying, say, an appliance, swarm together directly to the distributors in expectation of lower pricing. The magic of numbers worked.

The concept was brought to North America by one of my clients. We were engaged to create a feasibility study. Our conclusion was "no," it wouldn't work here because retailers were organized into powerful buying groups and wouldn't stand for being circumvented. We also envisioned that it would cause havoc with pricing at all levels of the vertical chain.

The swarm model was beta tested here and barely received a lukewarm reception by buyers and sellers alike.

Apparently, we, as consumers, are not fixated solely on price. In fact, the more we pay for a product such as a car, a home, or even a mammoth 84-inch television, the greater our bragging rights.

We are victims of a "snob appeal" mentality. Go figure.

Action Planning/Workbook

1. Do not simply abandon your opportunity because you are feeling lonely. Work to justify your concept.
2. Go back to your original Business Model. Look at your assumptions. Revisit your forecasts, revenue streams, and any other critical factors.
3. Ask for input. Talk to trusted associates and professionals. Gather advice and opinions. Determine what, if anything, needs to change or to be tweaked.
4. Develop your "Unique Selling Proposition" where and how you differentiate yourself from competitors. This involves being able to offer

customers something that the competition cannot or does not offer. Can your Business Model support that?

5. Is your position defensible? Prove it to yourself and any sounding board you trust.

6. Rebuild your Business Model to reflect any changes that will make it more acceptable to an identified market sector, and thereby more sustainable.

CHAPTER 8

Help Me Mr. Google

Highlights

People don't buy your "X-13 Mega Super Widget" because of who you are and why you sell it; they buy your product because of what it does for them. You are their "solution" (a very overused, over-flogged word). And market research helps you shape your product or service to meet the needs and expectations of your prospective customers.

The relationship you build with your target audience centers around WIIFM ("what's in it for me"). Your client is the "me" and has just sat through most of your elevator pitch or marketing presentation. They find an appropriate moment to interrupt you and say, "Yes, that's all very nice, but what does it do for me?" Market research helps you identify those hot buttons that buyers seek. They are the triggers that close deals.

You are not so much selling a product or service as you are selling a fix or a hope.

Actually, that's not quite 100 percent true. There is always a small, shallow group that buys because they simply have the need to own a piece of you, regardless of your usefulness to them. Or because of a spokesmodel or moderately literate sports hero they want to associate themselves with. Or it's just cool. It has no intrinsic value to them other than status, pride of ownership, and bragging rights. They collect bright, shiny "things," but they are not the mainstay of your market. They are the fringe.

Build your business around "need," not the "needy."

Why do market research? The real question should be: why wouldn't you?

The objective of your venture is to generate revenues in a certain marketplace to a chosen target market and prospective customer base and likely competing against others in a possibly already crowded playing field.

Not easy. Market research helps you rise to the challenge of identifying how you fit in, and what you must do to thrive.

- Know as much as you can about your market and marketplace.
- Research results can suggest how you must fine tune or tweak your products or services to meet the needs of those who may choose to deal with you.
- Gain confidence that your venture might very well succeed.
- Identify issues and challenges that may arise as you battle for recognition and market share.
- Market research can help you develop an effective brand and a clear message for your buying base. How you package, price, and promote your products or services is critical.
- Every successful business carries out ongoing market research. It's a good habit for you to get into, and it's a continual process as well. It must never stop.

Market Research

Remember that this is your first foray into carrying out market research. A future chapter ("Even More Market Research") will deal with "deep diving" your market research where you come down from the heavenly 50,000-foot view to explore gaps to fill and traps to avoid. And more hot buttons to push.

Look inwards. What prompted you to undertake this entrepreneurial quest? It was based on some assumptions, ideas, or insight. Go back and revisit those. Go to the source of your inspiration. See if they are still valid, and not just a "spur of the moment" decision based on that "How to Make a Million Overnight" article you saw in the supermarket rag sheet tabloid.

Here are some early-stage Market Research 101 "how to" basics, including a few tidbits they don't teach you.

- Ask potential customers. I had a client who wanted to set up a gluten-free bakery, but was uncertain about the market.

I had them prepare some samples and set themselves up adjacent to a local high-end bakeshop, offering goodies to try. While the tasters swooned with delight, they answered questions about taste, price, frequency of shopping, and even demographics. The point is: get creative and try to go to the people (or companies) you need to befriend.

- Mr. Google and his Internet cohorts (Safari, Edge) are likely the main source of information gathering. Check out competitor websites and social media pages. See how they package, brand, price, and promote. Ignore any testimonials. I can write as many as you need.

- The Internet never forgets. If you're looking up market stats, it will regurgitate websites that offer up data that is decades old. Be wary of old information, especially in our rapidly evolving times. I just looked up new electric car brands and got several hits about Henry Ford's Model T wonders. Seriously?

- While you're at it, try to cut through the fluff and fill that the Internet is famous for. Useless, irrelevant stuff. Focus on what is relevant to your research.

- Eliminate input extremes. People, websites, and reports lie. They do so to boast, create some sensationalism, or to scare competitors away.

- As far as trade and statistical reports and industry journals, the cliché is "figures don't lie but liars figure." Draw your own conclusions using the source data compiled and presented.

Hurdles

Don't believe in just what you want to believe. If your market research waves a few red flags, pay attention.

We tend to have some preconceived ideas of what our market research may uncover. Try to fight those impulses to predict outcomes. Don't crystal-ball based solely on wishful thinking.

Finally, your research needs to have a finish date, otherwise the process can go on forever. Set parameters to the research work. At some point, enough is enough, especially if you hear the same things over and over.

Tales From the Trenches

My associate and I are the founders of "Russkie Brewskie"©, a branded Russian beer. We thought it might have been interesting, especially during the early Trump–Putin love affair. We even had a photoshopped picture of the two riding together on a horse—bare chested. Remember, it was intended as a fad product.

We couldn't really understand why nobody had picked up on this brainstorm. My associate wanted to launch head first, but since I was heading overseas, I undertook to do some homework.

I met with some Russian breweries and discovered two reasons these Russian beers never made it to North America.

1. The beer itself looked and tasted like what Kevin Costner drank in Waterworld—recycled urine. It was putrid, and they were leery to change the recipe.
2. As soon as I mentioned licensing, the brewery owners joined the meeting. Well dressed and accompanied by ginormous bodyguards, the brewery facilities, apparently, were owned by the Russian Mafia.

I beat a hasty retreat, thankful that a modicum of caution and market research kept me from a watery grave in the Volga, as were the rumors circulating regarding other Russian–North American joint venture partners.

Action Planning/Workbook

1. From a market perspective, prepare a profile of your (proposed) Business Model and how you see it working.
2. List all the things about your venture's Marketing Plan that you are not certain about.
3. Carry out market and industry research based on the guidelines in this chapter.
4. Now, list everything that you are quite comfortable with regarding in your business.

5. Again, carry out market and industry research on these and try to identify where you may have been overconfident.

6. How has this Market Research 101 changed your version of the business, or has it? What may need some tweaking to increase its chances of success?

CHAPTER 9

Understand Your Competitors

Highlights

Those pounding footsteps you hear getting louder behind you are either your adoring fans or your competitors zeroing in on you. Even before you launch, or just when you do step into the marketplace limelight, you are being tracked.

In this global economic environment, your competitors may be thousands of miles and several continents away. Our big commercial world is getting smaller with every new platform that materializes (likely coded and developed by some 17-year-old wonder kid with braces and no social graces).

As you are planning your business, one of your important tasks is to identify who you will be up against. Most markets are limited in size, and nobody who is already entrenched in your sector will give up market share readily. One of your best resources is to know your "enemy."

Sun Tzu *wrote in his famous book,* The Art of War,

If you know the enemy and know yourself, you need not fear the result of a hundred battles.

—Fifth Century BC Chinese General

Business has also become a game of "leapfrog," particularly in crowded market environments where there is usually (almost always) someone faster, bigger, cheaper, with deeper marketing pockets and offering a slightly better product or service than you.

For the new or start-up entrepreneur, this can be a frightening prospect. However, you too can and should be playing the "understand your competitor" game.

It's more than knowing who's who. It's important to understand how your competitors operate in your markets, their successes, their failures, and their business models, that is, how they function (margins, supply chains if any, staffing, position in the market, in fact anything that you can use as a yardstick for your company).

Here's a shopping list of "must knows" regarding competitors.

- *How they market*
- *Pricing policies, discounts, and terms*
- *Distribution channels*
- *Degree of innovation over the years*
- *Staffing*
- *Media activities*
- *Profile of owner(s)*
- *Reputation*

Your information gathering vehicles, including those covered in an earlier chapter ("Help Me Mr. Google"), could include any of these avenues. And don't forget to put quotations marks around your Google search request. This will narrow down your searches.

- *Advertising they may do across all electronic, digital, and hard copy sources*
- *Visits to their place of business*
- *Trade magazines*
- *Networking, also referred to as "schmoozing," at conferences, trade fairs, or any social get-togethers.*

Competition goes beyond established players. There are upstarts continuously cropping up, and they can be as dangerous or even more so than the conventional competitors. Why? They are born hungry.

Hurdles

Stay current. Never let yourself fall behind in watching your competitors or identifying changes in the marketplace. Lose sight and you are lost.

There is no room for complacency. Never assume everything is just fine. The truth is, changes are ongoing. It can be subtle and still require you to adapt your product or service offerings, prices, policies, or promotional strategies.

Do not fear change. Embrace it. Build your Business Model with the ability to transition/pivot quickly and effectively.

Tales From the Trenches

There was a time in the growth of my consulting firm that I had outgrown my office space and searched available leased premises for a new home. With the office infrastructure I sought, there was nothing affordable in the location I wanted.

After extensive market research, I decided to build a shared resource business center in an existing lease space, with the offices and layout I wanted for my company, plus an additional dozen offices to rent out to others.

Traditionally, shared office space provides central reception and secretarial services, boardroom rentals, and telephone answering services. The shared space model provided sufficient revenues to cover my facility operating costs and then some.

The Business Model proved so successful that I repeated it for my several out-of-town offices.

In typical start-up junkie fashion, I sold my interests in the three business centers I had launched. I certainly fit the "build it–grow it–sell it" character of the entrepreneur who always seeks out the next shiny coin on the road.

Entrepreneurship is a grandiose adventure. Anything less is called a job.

Action Planning/Workbook

1. Find a business similar to the one you are launching or have just launched.
2. Role model. Put yourself in their place. Find out everything they do and how they do it. This book has several chapters devoted to information gathering and deep-diving market research strategies.

3. Put yourself on the mailing lists, blogs, and newsletters of your competitors.

4. Join, and be an active member of organizations that focus on your business sector.

5. Is there anything to add/delete/change regarding your proposed business? Revisit your Business Model regularly.

CHAPTER 10

Trend or Fad?

Highlights

Fads burst onto the scene, have instant uptake, and just as fast end up in your next garage sale or are thrown into a giveaway box. One hit wonders. Every generation has its own fad burdens to bear.

- *For Baby Boomers and late bloomer entrepreneurs, examples of fads are hula hoops, bolo bats, and the yoyo.*
- *For Gen Xers, bell-bottom pants, hippies, and disco likely elicit memories best filed away but never really forgotten. These were all part of you.*
- *For the casual-conscious Generation Y (Millennials), micromobility, designer beers, and self-care products accounted for some of the predominant uptakes.*
- *And for the current trend-setting Gen Z, that is, the COVID remote office generation, online shopping is predominant. Facebook Marketplace has a billion users and sells to 250 million consumers each month. TikTokMadeMeBuyIt has been viewed over 30 billion times. Online grocery sales accounted for 96 billion dollars, or 11 percent, of all grocery sales in the United States in 2020.*

Even in business, fads like open offices and management by committee have thankfully come and gone. Business trends, however, often become mainstays in business and the entrepreneurial culture. They get absorbed into the everyday. Get to know them.

In this chapter, fads and trends are discussed both from (1) a product and service perspective and (2) from a business and management viewpoint.

Why? Because in the formative stages of planning or preparing to launch your business. Understanding fads and trends can impact and influence not only what you bring to the market, but also how effectively you run your company.

Maybe there is something you can learn from those who have ventured before you, and you can judiciously avoid small enterprise "opportunity pitfalls" like vape shops and frozen yogurt franchises.

On a larger scale, let's not forget a recent fad inductee, Peloton, which predicted that health clubs' demise because of COVID had permanently changed our need for social interaction and human contact. Look where they are now! Exploiting a home exercise fad may prove highly detrimental for the company.

Even understanding larger-scale failures such as Kodak, Blockbuster, and Blackberry should teach you that "innovate or die" is more than a catchy phrase.

Learning From the Past Is a Vital Part of Your Journey Into Successful Entrepreneurship

The past is a place of reference, not a place of residence; the past is a place of learning, not a place of living.

—Roy T. Bennett, author

Products and Services

Products and Services Fad	Products and Services Trend
Fast appearance accompanied by significant media exposure, rapid uptake, and even faster disappearance	Interest in launching products and services that have market longevity and the ability to grow
Something that promises a quick fix (i.e., "You too can make millions almost overnight")	Morphable items that can act as the foundation for new offerings and can react to market changes
Far too good to be true, and generally are not	Can be genuinely warrantied and carry a credible guarantee of performance or services delivery
Very little backup support, such as studies or possibly promoted by a report produced by The University of Lower Albania or its equivalent	Delivers quantifiable results that are well documented and well received by customers/clients

Products and Services Fad	Products and Services Trend
Wrong, usually simplistic conclusions from studies, but nobody really cares. Seriously, nobody citing the misleading information really cares	Integrity is a selling feature for products and services. The buyers/users can feel comfortable that their expectations will be met

Business and Management

Business Fad	Business Trend
Ideas and practices that have marginal utility in your day-to-day workload	Dedication to customer service and satisfaction
Quick rise in sales followed by a Houdini-type disappearance	Sustainability of your Business Model
Better at raising hopes than delivering results	Team and staff built on talent and loyalty to the brand
Rarely challenge the status quo within the company structure because they are superficial in nature and applicability	Ability to react to changing conditions, including inflation, marketplace fluctuations, and supply chain insecurities
Not terribly novel. Often built on repackaging existing ideas and concepts that already have wide acceptance. This reduces their rejection rates	Involved in all sectors of the business and open to more as technology evolves
Questionable "gurucide" spokespeople, that is, highly remunerated business, sports or celebrity cheerleaders with self-proclaimed infamy and limited qualifications	Reactive to changing customer priorities such as sustainability and consumer consciousness
	Unrelenting market, trends, and competitor market tracking
	Genuine, over-the-top commitment to customers and clients
Short-term thinking. Returns based on instant gratification of fad revenues	

Hurdles

It is difficult and dangerous to build a venture based on a Business Model or products/services that are fad-oriented.

Fads are far more fast-payback and have a certain attraction to the restless entrepreneur. They, however, tend to give a false sense of elation in that the payback benefits fade quickly and the entrepreneur purveyors need to continuously find new offerings to flog. Try to avoid this direction for your business.

That having been said, there are entrepreneurs who thrive on fads, taking advantage of every quick-hit opportunity. Launching a product, for example, that offers an elixir to a market seeking an immediate fix can be rewarding as long as those businesspeople realize the temporary nature of their marketability. Fad diet supplements and instant success business training offering almost immediate returns are perfect examples of selling quick BS hits.

Trends, on the other hand, take more effort to package into a venture. But the longer-term paybacks outweigh any immediate limited "fad" gratification.

Tales From the Trenches

I was responsible for the design and implementation of an indigenous line of health care and giftware products. I spent a great deal of time and effort assuring authenticity and even engaged a number of indigenous communities' "knowledge keepers" to confirm that what we proposed to market was genuine. That was important to me.

My partners in the venture, however, were anxious to launch. Their interest in authenticity ended with the speedy marketing of the line. Content and genuine product makeup were decidedly secondary considerations.

We arrived at a compromise. I suggested they launch a second line under a different brand, and they could load in all the hype they wanted, as long as there was no association with the original core business. They agreed.

The secondary business they launched amidst great fanfare skyrocketed, but then settled onto the dusty shelves of airport gift shops and souvenir stores.

My core business was launched with far greater product credibility and with well-recognized indigenous spokespeople.

It thrived, and, once more, at the appropriate time and following my start-up junkie philosophy, I sold my interests.

There were other shiny coins on the road calling me.

Action Planning/Workbook

1. Are you a short-term or long-term thinker? Explain. Give five features to justify your choice.

2. Do your products or services have strong credibility and longevity factors? Give five reasons to justify your choice.

3. Will they be perceived as fads or trends? Give five reasons to justify your choice.

4. What are your short-term business goals? Do they fall within the fads or trends categories?

5. How important is instant gratification to your business goals? Explain.

6. Do the same for your long-term goals.

7. Once you have completed the aforementioned, use a trusted sounding board to present and discuss your responses. This will help set a direction for your proposed business. It is a very worthwhile exercise.

CHAPTER 11

Who Will Buy This/Use This?

Highlights

The very first questions funders will ask you is "Who will be your customers? Who will buy this?" This is what you need to ask yourself as well, and you had better have the answers before you launch.

If you want to instantly end a meeting or pitch with a funding manager or investor, just respond, "Everyone. Everywhere." Groans will quickly follow.

For purposes of clarification, a *target market* refers to a potentially large assembly of people or businesses with common features and needs that you may target in your Marketing Strategy. A *target audience* zeroes in. It is a subset of a larger target market and consists of a well-defined cluster group of consumers or businesses within the larger entity. Your goal is the target audience, a more approachable entity. Something you can quantify and get your arms around.

Your products or services need to focus down onto a specific marketplace: people, demographics, geographic location, types of companies, market sectors, and as much specificity as you can muster.

Any campaigns you launch need to be market specific. Even how you image your company should be geared to gain the interest and attention of a clearly defined sector of the public or a target corporate market.

That applies equally to dressing up your products or services into a recognizable and memorable package. Otherwise, you will get lost in the crowd of anonymity, a world where nobody really cares about you or recognizes what you do, or, worse yet, doesn't feel any urge to deal with you. Game over.

Assuming you do not have limitless funds, it is also important that any marketing you undertake can hit home and impact whomever you are trying to reach out to. That translates to generating revenues, not just "market curiosity." Cash flow is your lifeblood.

How Do You Determine Your Target Audience?

- Determine who your competitors are likely selling to, or appealing to on their website, social media, literature, and advertising. You then have the choice to copycat them, or ride on their coattails by using their market presence in your promotions (i.e., "We are like ABC Company, but better"), or find a gap that others in your competitive sector are missing. Fill that niche.
- Design the perfect client profile: age, profession, gender, geographic location, and buying habits.
- Conduct first-tier market research using all readily available sources.
  - Regional or community economic development/business offices who maintain data on businesses and activities in the region, business licenses issued, and other public domain databases.
  - Research competitive websites. You can generally get a "feel" for who they are appealing to and what they offer.
  - Interview people "in the know" and whom you can trust.
- Carry out "deep-dive" market research (also covered in this book "Deep Dive: Even More Market Research")
- Assimilate and review your findings, and see how close you come to your ideal client profile.
- Make sure your Marketing Strategy reflects your findings.

Hurdles

All of the above having been offered up, it is difficult to find out everything you want to. Set a reasonable timeline for this task and work with what you are able to compile.

Focusing down is key. Too many owners set their targets too broadly on larger target markets and thereby miss out on the more reachable client audience before their eyes.

Eliminate fluff or extremes from your info gathering. Look for commonality between your researched sources. Hearing or seeing the same results gleaned repeatedly from the research process adds credibility to the findings.

Tales From the Trenches

In launching my consulting practice, I engaged a market research firm to identify 35 of the most likely clients whom we could and should approach. This was based on a profile we had developed, our "ideal" customer.

The research firm came back with a list of 375 firms and organizations suitable as targets. Obviously trying to impress, but ignoring their directive. It was overpowering and decidedly nonimplementable for a company our size. After inquiring most facetiously if they created their research findings report by replicating an industry directory, I fired them.

I replaced the research firm with several of my own people working within a very specific and limited mandate.

I had set a goal of reaching and building a relationship with realistically no more than 20 companies. Any two or three would have given us a foothold market share sufficient for my start-up.

We secured two excellent clients by our launch date, and we were on our way.

Lesson learned: only mandate work to people you know, trust, and can control.

Action Planning/Workbook

1. Build a profile of your ideal customer, be it a person or another business.
2. Select the market research tools that are within your ability to undertake. What would those be?
3. Determine your bigger picture target market. What is it?

4. Focus down onto your more immediate and reachable target audience. What is it?

5. Contact information delivery sources, including community data compiled by the Chamber of Commerce and Economic Development/ Business Office.

6. Reach out to your target audience using media kits and surveys. This will help you focus on your prospective customer base.

7. Revisit your customer profile and target audience based on any findings that wander away from your expectations.

CHAPTER 12

The Deep Dive Into Competition Research

Highlights

Keep in mind that attaining market share means you are getting it from somewhere. That usually represents taking business away from competitors. How well do you know your competition? By now, you should have a pretty good idea of who you are up against. But how about their business strategy? How do they operate? Are they succeeding or faltering? What are their strengths and weaknesses? What do customers think about them? How can you inch in on their market share?

Deep diving delivers far greater insight into your competition, but also demands that you delve, probe, mine for nuggets, and plunge in to uncover gems of intelligence that can give you a competitive edge. Is it a legal activity? Yes, pretty much. Is it scrupulous? Mostly. Is it ethical? It may require some moral elasticity. Should you have any misgivings deep diving? Resoundingly "NO."

Deep diving asks a lot of you. Much of what you will seek out is accessible, but some aspects may be more difficult to access. You choose. It is best to carry out this task to whatever limits you set for yourself.

I, personally, have never had any issues in this regard. Perhaps my need to know has always exceeded any second-guessing of any ethereal standards of right and wrong.

There are a series of steps in competition deep-diving research that I can recommend.

Identify your competitors: This sounds like a pretty obvious starting point, but there is some finesse involved. Use as many search engines as you can and be specific in your search requests. When you see the same names cropping up in multiple lists, those are your obvious targets. Choose a small handful (5 or 10 max) and ignore the rest.

Background: Websites will often boast about ownership, products or services, years in business, position in the marketplace (i.e., "industry leader"), and organization (i.e., sales team, customer service department, and product development group). Check these out, but remember, they may well be embellished.

Facilities: Are their locations important to their business (i.e., high-traffic area) and are they impressive? Go for a visit and check them out.

Products and services: Find out what they offer to their customers. For product businesses, contact their order desk and gage their inventory stocking practices. Can you compete effectively with the extent of their offerings? Can you offer anything unique, that is, fill any identified gaps you see in their products or services?

Pricing: This is always iffy because businesses offer package deals, specials, high-priority client pricing, rebates, and other customer retention strategies. Your best bet is to set yourself up as customer and enter their world of pricing variables.

Marketing: This is probably the easiest component to research. Likely their marketing and promotion strategies are "out there" to see. Perhaps engage a marketing guru for a brief stint to analyze competitors' brands, technology delivery platforms, advertising, and any other vehicles being used by competitors to attract and maintain customers.

Reports: If any of your competitors are publicly owned companies, they will have produced annual reports which have a wealth of information ranging from financial results and developments in progress, to staffing. These reports are readily available.

Classify the competition: Based on all of the above, grade your competitors as "primary" (direct, similar to you), "secondary" (not quite the same as you but with offerings close to yours), or "tertiary" (same target market but different target audience). For start-up purposes, focus on the primary and concern yourself about the rest later.

Hurdles

There are three hurdles you will likely encounter.

1. Sorting through the marketplace to identify which competitors are most likely your major concern. The fear is that you are omitting a competitor who is evolving and growing to be someone worthy of your attention. Don't overthink. Stick with the obvious ones.
2. Some of the information you would like to access is simply not available—well concealed in the intellectual property vault of your competitors. While this may at first feel frustrating, just move on.
3. Information overload is a third challenge. Not only will you gather a fair amount of insight into your competitors, but sorting what is important will also be a test.

Tales From the Trenches

I had a wealthy investor in a freeze-drying technology company who was impatient to act. I am generally the opposite. Obviously, risk and money meant a great deal more to me than to him.

We had a working prototype, but were not quite there yet. It had limited capacity and throughput, and I did not want to reveal our secret to the public. The intellectual property was our only asset.

Mr. Money won out, but, at my strong insistence, we embedded the motherboards and a few other crucial components in tamperproof and impenetrable space-age black epoxy compounds.

We ended up launching before I thought we were fully ready. We succeeded because of our unique technology, which improved dramatically over time, as did our bottom line with every "new improved" rendition. Protecting the sensitive workings continued on as part of our company policy.

Action Planning/Workbook

1. Once you have carried out your "deep-dive" competition research, carry out a SWOT analysis ("strengths, weaknesses, opportunities, threats") of the competitors you have identified as primary.

2. Review the results carefully to determine where you may have a competitive advantage, and what competition features and offerings you have identified as dangerous to your business.

3. Include mitigating strategies in your master plan for dealing with anything that could endanger or erode your market entry and position.

4. Here's another important note: When you quote stats, trends, and opinions, back these up for your audience, including for yourself and possibly investors, with third-party sources. This kind of information sounds a lot better coming from someone else and not just from you.

CHAPTER 13

Growth Strategies

Highlights

It seems incongruous to talk about growth strategies when you are just learning to walk. After all, this book is geared to start-ups and early-stage businesses. For newbies, planning for the day after tomorrow is considered a growth strategy.

But I have learned that having a perspective on "where to from here" is a very valuable outlook to nurture. It is "end of the rainbow" thinking, the kind of outlook that fuels almost every planning decision you will make.

Growth strategies turn every entrepreneur into a visionary.

Here are the main categories and considerations to include in your growth strategy, remembering that your strategy is yours alone, conceived and developed by you, and in conjunction to where you see yourself and your business downstream. It's all about you.

- *At some point you will feel stifled by your market share. It was reasonable when you started your venture, but things are different now. Your growth strategy can be gaining more traction by maturing naturally, increasing your client base over time. Or you can adopt a more aggressive strategy.*
- *Expand your offerings beyond your current menu of products or services. This is called "organic growth," where you capitalize on your internal resources to encourage growth. Develop brand new products and services that should be of interest to your existing customer base. Make sure that your current clients are likely customers for your new offerings.*

- *Diversify by vertical integration to your existing line(s). For example, the marketing company adds a web graphic design team or a media group.*
- *Acquiring competitors to increase market share. Your interest would primarily be their client base and their brands.*
- *Establishing branch offices outside your current geographic marketplace.*
- *Form cooperatives or license agreements where others operate under your corporate umbrella.*
- *Creation of strategic partnerships whereby you joint market or enter into other joint initiatives with others who compliment but do not compete directly with you.*

You surely must be getting excited at the prospects. But how do you accomplish this?

1. Build on your core business. After all, you already have a customer base in your sights. What else can you offer them over and above what you will originally provide? Build on customer satisfaction. Maintain customer loyalty. Existing clients are an important building block for growth and diversification.
2. Limit the risk factor related to any growth strategy.
3. Stay flexible, adaptable to changing markets, demographic shifts, evolution of new identified needs and changes, large and small, in your marketplace. Be ready to act at all times.
4. Reinvest profits into growth. Not all of the profits. You need to pay yourself, but limit extravagancies like a luxury lifestyle until you have earned it.
5. Continually build your brand and market awareness. Everything you build should reflect that brand.
6. Stay abreast of your competitors, and don't allow others to simply leapfrog your position in the market because you resist change. Remain reactive.

There are four interesting categories of growth strategies for small business (*Technology Management Review* May 2012). How do you classify yourself, keeping in mind that one is not superior to the others? They vary primarily in their aggressiveness and tolerance/intolerance for risk.

1. *Exploit*—market-oriented profit makers and business rebuilders, capitalize on high-risk opportunities such as acquiring companies in trouble and selling off its assets.
2. *Restrain*—often referred to as downsizers who are control oriented, overly cautious, and content with incremental growth.
3. *Expand*—growth-oriented entrepreneurs who thrive on expanding their existing business. The majority of entrepreneurs fall within this category.
4. *Explore*—the radical innovators and opportunity explorers. The Steve Jobs of the business world. Find a niche to thrive in.

Hurdles

The most significant hurdle, particularly for start-ups or early-stage businesses, is that growth strategies may seem removed and rather far away from the day-to-day grind it takes to run your business. They can seem like fantasies.

The other predominant hurdle is "over or under-dreaming," that is, aiming too low or too high. That is understandable since the fledgling entrepreneur has little frame of reference about what the future may bring.

Don't let these stop you from dreaming, where those visions represent ranges rather than specific targets.

Tales From the Trenches

When I planned the launch of my consulting practice, I had great expectations for the future. My literature and website boasted of a family of expert services and a team approach. To the uninitiated, it appeared that I was spearheading a group of exceptional professionals.

All of this was implied in my promotional and marketing materials. However, I was a one-man show.

I never lost sight of where I wanted to be in five years' time. I hired the best I could afford and delegated responsibilities. I took on a competent partner who shared my goals, possibly with even more proactive growth strategies than me.

Over the years, we initiated our growth plans, assuring one had taken root before moving on to the next.

Once I had realized my vision for the firm, I sold my interests.

Alas, the soul of a start-up junkie is a wandering spirit.

Action Planning/Workbook

1. Define your business dreams three and five years down the road.
2. List what you think needs to be accomplished to achieve those dreams.
3. Build a timeline and a milestones chart as to what needs to be accomplished at each step before moving on.
4. Frame it for visibility and keep it where you can see it every day. Let your growth strategies become your mantra.
5. Leave your options open to take a more aggressive stance, especially if new growth opportunities present themselves.
6. Keep a log of alternate business opportunities that cross your path.

CHAPTER 14

The Joys of Branding

Highlights

When you were young(er), you had a certain style about you. How you dressed. How you came across to others. How you interacted with people. That was your brand. It defined you.

In business, your brand tells your story. It is the grown-up version of you. It's what you stand for. Same principle. Higher stakes.

Your brand is a commitment to your customer/client base. It is an assurance of quality, consistency, and value, and has huge meaning in the marketplace. It offers an ambitious, aspirational promise that evokes emotion. It is supported by a strong operational plan to consistently deliver that promise.

> *Your brand is what people say about you when you're not in the room.*
>
> —Jeff Bezos, CEO, Amazon

How Exactly Do You Develop a Brand?

Start with a memorable name: Considering the viewers' average digital attention span is 8 to 10 seconds, your name needs to convey your brand's message instantly. Don't get too cutesy. Choose something that will garner a second look from prospective clients.

The purpose of your brand: This is the core creative process. Ask yourself why your customers should care about you. What do you want them to know about you? What, if anything, makes you (semi-)unique?

Competitors: How are your competitors positioning themselves in the marketplace? What are their branding strategies? Can you improve on that messaging for your own company and your products and services?

Touching your target audience: Branding is target audience-specific. Once you have determined your buying audience, you can focus your messaging to them, and them alone.

Develop a personality for your brand: Decide if your brand personality will be highly serious, playful, inviting your audience on an adventure, or decidedly solution-based, simply meeting their identified needs, mundane or otherwise. Whatever you decide should come across in any messaging you present to the market.

You need a story: A good brand will connect emotionally to your clients. What enticed you to start your business? Any stories about the journey? People are buying your story as much as your offerings.

Create a memorable visual identity: It needs to be something simple, easy to recognize. It needs to adorn everything you produce and every piece of digital or hard copy marketing, newsletters, blogs, web updates, and advertising that you generate.

Let's Discuss the Dos and Don'ts of Branding

- *Do not get hung up on logos and slogans*. They are not brands. They are just marketing messages that support your brand. Logos and slogans are 2 percent of marketing, but 98 percent of local attention goes to them. You do not choose Ford over Chevy because of their logo or slogan.
- *A brand is a perception*. A brand is what people think of you, not what you say you are. We create them through visual cues, people and attitudes, word of mouth, publicity, advertising, and social media. Good brands sell a feeling, not a place or a product.
- *Successful brands have a narrow focus*. You cannot be all things to all people. Promote your authentic core. Do not do what everyone else is doing just because they are doing it. Do not just market what you have; market what will close the sale.
- *Bring your brand to the market when you can deliver on the promise*. Brands are earned, good or bad.
- *Great brands always need a plan*. What do you want to be known for? What do you need to do to own the brand? How will you deliver your message?

Hurdles

Branding is a process. Many entrepreneurs tend to rush through it all without realizing how significant and impactful the outcome can be.

Another issue that arises is that your brand may not be appropriate for the demographics of your target audience. I have seen products packaged for the young marketed to baby boomers and beyond. It doesn't work. Think carefully about who you are selling to.

Beta test your brand—a worthwhile exercise is to ask people what they think of when you present your brand and logo. What response does it elicit? It's easier to change or tweak your brand in its formative stage.

Tales From the Trenches

One of my clients was a significant importer of Indian foods and spices. He was in the process of developing a new brand and sought my advice. My three questions to him were, "why do you want to rebrand, who do you sell to now, and are you seeking a new target audience with this rebranding?"

Their current market was the Indian ethnic community, but, with increased interest in Indian cuisine, the company wanted to reach out to the nonethnic community as well.

The name they chose for their new branded line was "Maha," Indian for "mighty and illustrious." It also happens to be the name of a Bollywood action-romance movie, which might explain the appeal to my client. I've never watched it. Nobody I asked had ever heard of it.

The new logo for this line was to be the calligraphic version of the name, very pretty, but totally marketing-meaningless.

To my clients, this all seemed appropriate. It had significance to them, but zero awareness or connection to their new intended target audience.

I set about to organize several focus groups where "Maha" and other suggestions were presented. The owners were surprised at the blasé reactions to "Maha."

I helped them develop a sub-brand for this new line, which proved to be quite successful.

The lesson here is that your brand needs to be entirely geared to your target audience, not you. They are your buyers. Connect with them.

Action Planning/Workbook

The content of this chapter is purposely designed to include the "how to" steps of the branding process and the importance of each stage. Please use it as your actionable items.

However, it all starts with introspection and reflection, and that is what is suggested herein.

- *Who are you? Sounds very metaphysical, but what I mean is how do you want to be perceived in the marketplace?*
- *What message do you want to portray to your customers?*
- *How do your chosen name, tag line message, and logo reflect who you are?*

Remember, it's your public that needs to be pleased, not you.

CHAPTER 15

Capture Customers

Highlights

Question: Where do your customers hang out? *Answer*: At your competitors.

The customers you are (or will be) seeking are already buying from your competitors. Logically, these are the first ones you want to go after. They are the "lowest hanging fruit." This needs to be part of your "Customer Attraction Battle Plan" ("CABP").

Call it "capture" or "attract" or "pilfer"; you need to find customers, especially during your formative business launch. Your competitors represent a bountiful hunting ground.

It's a back and forth battle as customers/clients will move between you and your competitors based on price, quality, service, loyalty, and other indefinable reasons such as goodwill, inertia, or simply an abhorrence (or desire) to change.

Once you launch, your competitors will obviously have your client base in their sites too, so just be ready to play the game.

You need a battle plan.

You should be creating your battle plan *before* you launch your business. It is a vital component that needs to be ready when you open your doors.

The strategies within your battle plan should also be part of your very makeup, the principles by which you and your people will govern yourselves. This behavior will reflect who you are and what you stand for— your core values. Part of your brand. Your customers and the marketplace will take note.

- Focus on smaller, not bigger niches. You can likely control a smaller market and carve out a competitive edge in doing something better than others.

- Stay current and relevant. Stay on top of industry trends and a step ahead of competition. Make it a component of your CABP to lead.
- Your customers are your business. Sometimes companies forget that it's the client who indirectly pay the staff salaries (and yours) and overheads. Don't lose sight of that, and make sure your people acknowledge this. Customers first.
- Build an organization that listens. Those working with you, for you, and customers themselves often offer suggestions for innovation and improvement. Make it a priority to listen.
- Do not be afraid to get "personal." Customers like stories, and yours is likely an interesting one. Join conversations. Confident entrepreneurs open up. Let people get to know you and not just your logo or offerings.
- Be prepared for price wars. Line up suppliers who would be willing to join the battle for customers by lowering costs. People like deals.
- Plan your growth strategy early on. Decide on any of these three goals: (1) growth "organically," from within the company, by increasing sales/revenues activity or (2) by adopting a policy of "growth by diversification," adding products/services to your offerings, or (3) "growth by acquisition," that is, buying competitors. The latter will allow you to grow dramatically and control a greater market share. However, this will also require an investment pool to be in place or accessible to you in order to carry out this objective. Work to secure this access to funding in your firm's early days.

Hurdles

Capturing customers is one of those areas you need to plan for even when you may not yet have any clients. Kind of a "cart before the horse" situation, but it's critical to design and implement a workable pathway to harvest customers and build a base. Start your CABP early on as part of your Business Plan.

Get past any squeamishness you may feel when we talk about capturing, borrowing, or absconding with competitors' clients. Assume the market is finite, and the pie that is currently divided up among existing companies in your sector is spoken for. The wedge you will work to extract must come from somewhere.

For example, a new restaurant that opens is soon packed with customers. Where did they come from? What other eateries are paying the price of the new eatery's entry into the arena?

Tales From the Trenches

It's not always a battle. One strategy that has worked for me is identifying complimentary companies, that is, those companies who served the same customer base I wanted to pursue, but marketed products or services differently from mine.

As an example, I applied this strategy when I was launching a health care product. I struck a revenue-sharing arrangement with a distributor who stocked the health care shelves at a major pharmacy chain with his own products that were complimentary to, but did not compete with mine. Win–win.

In another instance, I arranged a team to conduct short retail surveys at the entrance to competitors' stores. The results were threefold: (1) the survey gave us perspective to build a customer profile, demographics, needs, and other valuable insights (2) gathered names of prospective customers for our future promotional activity, and (3) handed out discount cards for the new business as a "thank you" gesture.

Action Planning/Workbook

This goes hand-in-hand with the "market and competition analysis" you would have already completed within this 30-Step Playbook and Workbook.

1. List five of your major competitors.
2. Carry out a competitive analysis. Compare their products and services to yours. How are you both the same? Different? Build on the differences?

3. How is their reputation for quality? Value of products/services? Customer support and satisfaction? List five of their saleable features.

4. Try to profile their customers. Who are they? Why do they deal with your competitors?

5. List five ways you can capture their customers.

6. What would you do to capture others' customers/clients? Your ethics may dictate your strategies.

CHAPTER 16

Numbers Crunching

Fun With Figures

Highlights

Budgeting and forecasting: You either hate or fear it, but you know how important it is as part of determining your business' viability. These may be the most tedious but important components of your planning and will most certainly be some of the key deciding factors when you reach your "go/no go" decision intersection.

Just plod on and do it.

Anticipating your future needs, spending, profits, and cash flow reveals where you are going and what to expect when you get there. Fewer surprises are a good thing.

Budgeting is often referred to as setting out a roadmap in numbers. Before you can make money, you have to figure out how you will spend it. It may also let you spot problems before they mushroom, such as how much money you need to launch your venture so that you can prepare accordingly and possibly switch gears.

A budget can be used as an internal tool for planning and monitoring the health of your business or as an external tool to demonstrate the viability of your business to funders, granting agencies, banks, investors, and/or partners.

Forecasting (budgeting) is often also referred to as a "What If," mainly because once you complete a draft of your budget, you can change any of the revenue or cost numbers to see how your venture can yield different results in different situations.

There are basically three types of budgets:

1. **Start-Up Budgets** to establish how much money you would need **before** you actually start generating any revenues. This would typically include "hard costs" such as equipment, computers, and furniture, and "soft costs" as represented by website development, legal, accounting, and, of course, working capital to pay monthly bills and costs as you start to build your enterprise.

2. **Operating Budgets**, which must clearly demonstrate how much revenue to expect to generate and what your related costs will be. Your Operating Budget would include estimating your revenues, cost of sales, labor, gross margins, and operating costs to run your venture.

   Costs would also include, but not be limited to, loan reimbursements, lease costs, materials, insurance, rent, marketing expenses and administrative costs, and other operational related cash-outflow items. Operating costs would only include "cash out" items, meaning that depreciation on equipment and suchlike would not be considered.

3. **Cash Flow Budgets** are designed to show monies in and monies out of a business. Why is this necessary? Your revenues may be seasonal and impact on your ability to generate cash on a timely basis. Your collections of what your clients owe you might take longer than your need to pay suppliers and overheads like electricity, rent, leases, or other items that are scheduled as payments. The net effect of all this determines what Line of Credit your business may need.

Let's look at a few forecasting scenarios that could be useful. If you are not yet familiar with them, you probably should be.

Gross Margin versus Markup: You will often hear the terms used interchangeably, but they are different, and it is important to understand that. A product, for example, sells for $30.00. Your cost is $20.00, so the profit is $10.00. That does not change, but how that is expressed does change. The $10.00 profit as a percentage of the $30.00 selling price represents a 33 percent *Gross Margin*. The $10.00 profit as a percentage of the cost represents a 50 percent *markup*.

Break Even: This is the expression of how much (or little) you need to generate in revenues to show a zero profit. In other words, how much revenue do you need to create to just cover your fixed costs?

Burn Rate: If you generated $0 in revenues, how much cash would it take to cover the cost of keeping your doors open? This is different from your "Break Even" level as the "Burn Rate" assumes there are zero revenues being realized. This is often a term used by investors who want to determine their cash outlay risk factor.

Hurdles

Quite often, funders may request that you prepare three budgets: worst case, normal (expected) case, and most optimistic case. Therefore, the "What If" name fits the budgeting process.

For start-up ventures, cash is generally tight. Budget for four to six months of low (if any) salary or draws and marginal income is commonplace. Knowing this and building it into your budget makes it more realistic.

Finally, understand that a budget is a living, breathing organism. It will change over time as your business does. It needs attention. Once you start in operation, revisit your budget quarterly or semi-annually. Compare it to your business's actual performance and update it to reflect any changes.

Tales From the Trenches

I was once asked to prepare a five- to seven-year forecast. At this time, I was dealing with this new financial institution's requirement, but my funding prospects look like they were likely panning out elsewhere. I could not take this new request for a "forever and ever" budget very seriously.

I submitted a multi-three-year proforma, and then noted "Year 4, Closer to Easy Street," "Year 5, Setbacks Caused by World Economic Downturn," "Year 6, Thinking of Retirement," "Year 7, Busy Working on My Tan Far Away." Not terribly clever, I know, but I could not help it.

Seriously, anything beyond a three-year forecast is star gazing.

I was tersely rejected by the new funder, but not dejected. (In hindsight, although it was funny, it was a somewhat impish act since I rarely burn bridges.)

In the same light, I had a tech client who submitted a Business Plan to me that basically called for world domination. His revenues model went from five million in year one to six billion in year five, and then quadruple again in year 10. As my consulting business grew, I used that as a "don't do this" teaching guide with my staff consultants. It never failed as an "ice breaker."

And the tech client? To my surprise, he found a "vulture capital" investor and managed to take his company public in a Pink Sheet RTO (Reverse Take Over). He became a millionaire on paper but could not dispose of his vested shares before the stock plunged from $1.75 to $.02 per share. It was a brilliant example of "reverse wealth." He is much happier now working as a barista.

The vulture capital investor, however, did very well, merrily shorting the stock he was manipulating.

Action Planning/Workbook

There is no shortage of budget and forecasting templates, from the very simple models to the highly complex prototypes that deal with multiple formulae and "what if" options.

For the planning that will help you get to your "go/no go" decision, I recommend a budgeting tool that walks you through every phase and line item in your forecast and forces you to make critical assumptions along the way. It is called "Liveplan." I would suggest that you visit www.liveplan.com.

Otherwise, you can use Mr. Google to identify other budget templates, including but not limited to SBA's (U.S. Small Business Administration) business guide and budget worksheets at www.sba.gov/business-guide or even BDC's "Entrepreneur's Toolkit" at www.bdc.ca/en/articles-tools/entrepreneur-toolkit.

CHAPTER 17

Start-Up Needs

Highlights

Planning and launching a new business is a soaring balloon ride. A fulfillment in waiting. But it's time to peel away a few layers of gushing endorphins and excitement and let the real-world creep in.

What will it cost you before you even open your doors? Let's take a closer look.

Your start-up costs, other than some hard assets, are very high risk. This is money you need to spend before you generate a single dollar. Before the first order or contract materializes. Before you even know if you will succeed or how long it will take you to flourish.

The following chart presents a reasonably comprehensive list of your start-up costs. Not all items will apply to you, but for those that do, carry out research and guestimate the costs. You need to know. Be conservative is estimating your costs.

The start-up costs are divided into four categories.

1. *One-time expenditures*: those nonrepeating costs prior to launching your venture.
2. *Hard assets*: everything from computers and furniture, to trucks.
3. *Building inventories* and prelaunch operating costs: stockpiling inventory, components, supplies as they may apply to your type of business.
4. *Surprises*: because there are always surprises.

Item	Guestimated Cost
ONE-TIME EXPENDITURES	
Legal fees	
Office space rent deposit	

(Continues)

(*Continued*)

Item	Guestimated Cost
Office leasehold improvements	
Licenses and permits	
Public utility deposits	
Website and social media	
Prelaunch advertising	
Business license	
Memberships and dues	
Incorporation costs	
Consultants (i.e., marketing, organizational planning)	
HARD ASSETS	
Computers, software, and accessories	
Furniture and fixtures	
Workstations	
Copier, scanner, printers	
Fork lifts, palletizers	
Display counters	
Showroom	
Phones, phone system	
Rolling stock	
BUILDING INVENTORIES, AND MORE	
Materials and components	
Equipment spare parts, repair items	
Packaging materials	
Insurance	
Printed supplies, promotional materials, exhibit displays	
Office supplies	
SURPRISES	
Working capital to carry you through the first "x" slow months	
Your salary and draws	
Management and bank loan administration fees	
Liability insurance	
Signage	

Item	Guestimated Cost
Taxes	
Accounting fees	
Prelaunch staffing needed	
Partnership agreement	
Copyrights and trademarks	

Other than leasing or financing hard assets, the risky nature of start-up costs, many of which are nonrecoverable should things go sideways, makes accessing start-up funds problematic. Some creativity is called for.

- Use your own money, but under one proviso: never mortgage the house, kids, and dog. The stress and risk factors are daunting.
- "Love" money, that being funding from family and friends, as long as you can accept being indebted to those close to you.
- Investors willing to take a minority interest. Be cautious what you offer for their participation.
- Crowdfunding, which has proven so successful in attracting strangers' interest, and cash inflow, but it is a slow process.
- Bank line of credit, excluding the use of high-interest credit cards.

Hurdles

There is a tendency for the budding, confident entrepreneur to overspend.

- Restrain yourself. Wherever possible, defer costs until your cash flow allows it.
- Avoid buying that Tesla until you have earned it.
- Think first and foremost about the business and avoid expenditures not directly related to launching your venture or generating early revenues.
- Remember that "OPM" (other people's money) has a cost, including obligations and possibly restrictions on how you run your business.

Tales From the Trenches

The arrogance and invulnerability of some new entrepreneurs is always entertaining. At one of my training workshops, I had one attendee who was convinced of her pending foregone brilliant success.

Armed with rich family money, this conceited young woman intended to open five luxury brand accessory stores simultaneously. She had her supply chains, locations, and staffing already hired. She was reckless. All she was missing was business acumen which money alone cannot guarantee.

Her efforts included trying to sell franchises even before there was a proven successful operating flagship.

She came to me in a frenzy about six months after the training workshop. She was in turmoil. Nothing was going right. She had way overextended herself and daddy was threatening to turn off the cash taps.

I taught her the concept of "baby steps" while I helped her draw back to a controllable business venture with only a couple of locations, less staffing, better marketing, and no more wasteful franchising effort.

She survived, but just. It must have been a humbling experience for her to realize that she too was only human.

Action Planning/Workbook

1. Assess your start-up needs. Be practical but frugal in your thinking.
2. Use the chart included in this chapter to guestimate your start-up funding needs.
3. Investigate the sources of start-up funding suggested herein, or any other avenue you can possibly approach.

CHAPTER 18

Pause for a Checkup Report

Welcome to the "pregnant pause."

You are a little over halfway through your 30-Step Playbook and Workbook journey. How are you doing? Are you getting closer to reaching the "go/no go" crossroads in deciding on the future direction of your entrepreneurial aspirations? Or, still somewhat ambivalent?

This is the ideal point in time for you to review and reflect and catch your breath. I know the voyage can be an arduous one.

Hopefully your decision making has been made easier by the legion of topics raised to date in the Playbook; the "how to/why to" presented for each step; the possible hurdles identified, and; the Action Planning/ Workbook laid out in a step-by-step format.

And, finally, the "Tales From the Trenches" hopefully lightened your load. You realize that you are not alone in living out these business adventures.

You deserve a breathing space, a time to validate, tweak, or possibly reshape your business roadmap.

Your next task is to complete the ***Checkup Report.*** There is no scorecard involved. This is an opportunity to journalize your thoughts.

Food for Thought	Your Notes
Have a solid vision of the Business Model you intend to pursue?	
Has your idea gone through several revisions? If yes, why were updates/changes necessary? What was the impetus to do so?	
Have you documented your early thoughts on your opportunity? Are they still valid today? Why or why not?	
Did you start off ambivalent about your business idea? More toward the "go" instead of the "no go"? How about now?	

(Continues)

(*Continued*)

Food for Thought	Your Notes
Do you feel that flexibility is part of your approach and mental makeup? Why or why not? Is it helping or hurting your planning process?	
Did you carry out competition research? Identified the key competitors you would face?	
What have you learned from your competition research? Are the results favorable/ supportive of your initiative?	
Have you analyzed the market itself and the trends?	
Comfortable with where this market is going? Sufficient stability?	
Did you build an ideal customer profile?	
Does the profile fit with the competition research you have done?	
Are you comfortable with the concept of working to capture, or even "steal" competitors' clients?	
Is there an identified and proven need for your product/service? How can that be justified to others, for example, funders, investors, partners?	
Identified a company similar to yours who can serve as your role model in shaping your own business?	
Anything you provide that would make you unique? Give you a competitive edge?	
Have you found and used a trusted sounding board for your idea?	
Does their feedback parallel your thinking? Conflict?	
Developed a brand for your business?	
Gotten feedback on your brand ideas? Will it work? Be recognizable? Build awareness in the market?	
Calculated your start-up and launch costs?	
Identified where you will secure funding for the venture?	

Food for Thought	Your Notes
Made any initial funding inquiries? Approaches? Inroads? What reaction did you get? Need to modify your 'ask'?	
Do you feel this is an affordable risk for you? How about for others who might have invested?	
Do you have the personal financial resources to put toward the business?	
Do you have a Plan "B" if this business does not work as you expect it to?	
At this stage, how is your comfort level with implementing your plan?	
Is your life-partner and/or family being supportive? Not just afraid to hurt your feelings?	
Is there any past entrepreneurial experience or training that you may have found helpful in the process?	
Are you at a point where you are (1) ready or (2) almost ready or (3) not ready to make a "go/no go" decision?	

Once completed, there are three *Action Planning/Workbook* items suggested.

1. *Review your work. Change any responses that needed a rethink.*
2. *Use a trusted sounding board/mentor to evaluate your Checkup Report and create a dialog with them.*
3. *Ready to continue on the balance of your journey through the 30-Step Playbook and Workbook with a greater vision and perspective of what you are striving to achieve?*

Tales From the Trenches

I have witnessed several early-stage companies proceed at full speed without carrying out the kind of planning, research, self-assessment, and introspection that is recommended in this book. The outcome of this arrogance can be fatal.

In one instance, I witnessed a technology platform company that was convinced beyond doubt that Blackberry was the future of cellphones and the iPhone was "another Steve Jobs ego trip" as they put it. They committed all their resources toward Blackberry apps. Their blinders were firmly in place and their beliefs were unshakable, even during Blackberry's decline.

Further, the founders invested heavily, personally, in fear of outsiders (investor, banks) owning their Intellectual Property. Their personal financial risk factor was high, but they seemed undeterred.

Did I mention that they did have a sounding board mentor, but he was a former Blackberry executive? Go figure. You've got to admire the blind leading the blind into the quicksand.

Several years of success were followed by a breakneck decline of their fortunes as Blackberry faded into the cellphone graveyard of obscurity.

The lessons here are ridiculously obvious; do your homework, then do it again; don't jump headlong into an opportunity when walking steadily into it will work just as well; choose impartial proven mentors, and always, always have a Plan "B."

I have often been asked how long the entire process should take. My response has always been "it takes what it takes." There are no rules, no deadlines, and no set timelines. You will simply know.

CHAPTER 19

Regulatory, Legalities, and Licensing

Highlights

Often overlooked and always the source of annoyance and frustration, issues such as licensing, certification, liability, compliance, regulatory agencies, and, dare I say it, taxes, can impact on your business planning process.

They eat up your time and attention. However, they represent the albatross business must deal with. For the new or soon-to-be-new enterprise, they are an important consideration.

As you continue your journey toward your "go/no go" decision, you must take the time to assure that these millstones can and will be dealt with and that none represent a looming obstacle to your plans.

Which of these apply to you? Because every community, region, state, or governing jurisdiction may have different demands, the categories below are somewhat generic. It is incumbent upon you to fit within your proposed business sector and location.

Please don't get alarmed. At this stage, it is a matter of assuring yourself that what is applicable to you is also accessible to you, and without great cost or inconvenience.

- Incorporation
- Business license
- Location zoning restrictions
- Name registration
- Business number
- Collection and payment of sales taxes
- Local and municipal improvement taxes

- Product/service liability insurance coverage
- Trade tariffs
- Import license
- Export license
- Compliance with trade restrictions
- Payroll wage rates guidelines
- Minimum wage standards
- Tax and source deductions collection and payment
- Environment compliance (if any)
- Hazardous materials standards and compliance (if any)

Hurdles

Understanding what areas you need compliance is a tedious but important undertaking. It is best to engage a compliance expert to walk you through it. Being aware and forewarned can add to your comfort zone.

Tales From the Trenches

I had an excellent working relationship with another consulting firm who had a spotless performance record over the course of their 10 years in business.

There was an opportunity for us to jointly bid on a large and complex contract whereby our combined synergistic areas of expertise could have been advantageous to us both as proponents.

The bid proposal called for each bidding party to provide proof of performance liability insurance. Although my firm had coverage, the co-bidder did not, and decried the need for the same since he had never experienced any backlash or difficulty.

I declined to co-bid with them, and they secured another party with whom to enter a joint proposal. They won the contract. The liability requirement clause in the ensuing consulting agreement was not enforced.

Unfortunately, the contract delivery ran into problems arising from the "contract management by committee" approach of the client. Then began the finger-pointing.

Liability issues came into play. It did not end nicely.

Liability conflicts can stop you in your tracks and drain your resources.

Action Planning/Workbook

1. There are a number of applications and software packages that provide compliance tracking tools, guides, and checklists. These might be worth exploring. Simply type "business compliance checklist" into Mr. Google, Safari, or any other web search platform.
2. Determine which of the listing agencies (and any others you may be aware of) apply to your planned business.
3. Identify the respective governing bodies.
4. Familiarize yourself with the requirements and registration processes.
5. Make phone calls to any entity where there is ambiguity or a requirement for further clarification. Try to make a "friendly gatekeeper" at the respective agency or agencies. Gatekeepers get stuff done!
6. Take meticulous notes regarding any conversations, e-mails, or personal contacts made. You will need these for later if and when you launch. Besides, this type of "CYA" provides a safety net for you.

CHAPTER 20

A Very Personal Perspective

Highlights

As you navigate the pathway toward deciding whether to launch your business or not, your personality will impact your decision-making process. Who you are, how you think, and what you believe in will play crucial roles in directing your actions.

We are the sum total of our beliefs. It sounds very Freudian, I know, but this *30-Step Start-Up Junkie's Playbook and Workbook* you are immersed in is exploring everything that goes toward your "go/no go" business launch decision. Your beliefs are a significant portion of the driving force. They are worth exploring.

See if you recognize yourself here. Characteristics and personality traits that great entrepreneurs share include, but are not limited to, the following. The more you identify with, the greater the chances that you will be especially diligent in pursuing your golden business opportunity.

- You demonstrate discipline in everything you undertake, completing tasks and diligently pursue results.
- Resilience in dealing with the unforeseen that always rears its head at the untimeliest occasions.
- Understanding others' motives and situations; being empathetic.
- Obviously, confidence is a major trait portrayed to others around you, including your staff.
- Innovative; the ability to try to stand apart, heads above others, and the desire to do so. This goes hand-in-hand with curiosity.
- Being a self-starter, taking on projects and tasks with a somewhat cautious but fearless demeanor.

- Able to change and adapt, and appreciate that change is not always a bad thing, such as shifting your business to parallel changing markets and fluctuating customer needs.
- The ability to communicate your thoughts, wants, and needs, and being a skilled and comfortable networker in any group situation.
- Resilience to absorb the blows, hiccups, and setbacks that business doles out.
- Entrepreneurship is a passion, and having that feeling of loving what you are doing is crucial for the survival of your business foray.
- Knowing who you are, your limits and abilities, demand a certain self-awareness and appreciation of your goals and vision.
- Resourcefulness, coupled with persuasiveness; knowing what you need, where to get it, who you may need to approach, and how to coax others to yield the results you are after.
- Leadership traits that motivate others to follow you, respect you, and do your bidding. Good leadership demands compassion as well and being respectful of others.

There are more characteristics and traits, but if you can fulfill the ones presented in this chapter, then you have all the makings of a diehard entrepreneur. Your "go/no go" business start-up decision will be facilitated by your inherent abilities, confidence, and common sense perspective.

Hurdles

Self-assessment is often a problematic task. We often think of ourselves in the best of terms, or our insecurities run rampant and we do not acknowledge some of our better attributes.

I suggest that after you undertake your own appraisal, you engage with someone who knows you, who has dealt with you, preferably in a business or work environment. Let them be the judge of your business-appropriate characteristics and personality as well.

You may find the comparison an enlightening experience.

Tales From the Trenches

There is such a thing as being too nice in business. Others may often perceive that as a sign of weakness.

On more than one occasion, I have seen clients and close associates who were not only decidedly nice people, but also projected these over-the-top niceties in their business dealings.

In many of these cases, they took on subservient roles in business relationships. They were often taken advantage of or assumed to be somewhat forceless and easily intimidated.

My rallying cry with the people has always been "You are too nice. Toughen up, at least in how you deal with others in business. You don't need to be impolite or rude. Just don't let others use you as a floor mat."

Niceness often oozes timidity and vulnerability in others' eyes, and is not ideal characteristic in you building a business or deciding whether entrepreneurship is your calling.

Action Planning/Workbook

1. In the listing of features and attributes, which ones do you feel best describes you?
2. Set up a score card listing all the features offered up in this chapter. Rate yourself as a 1 (this does not really describe me) to 5 (this is exactly who I am).
3. For the items with the higher scores (4 and 5), can you use these as the foundation to build your business persona?
4. For the items with lower scores (1 to 3), is there a possibility for you to deal with these possible shortcomings? After all, forewarned is forearmed.
5. In some instances, who you need to be in business is not who you are outside the business world. There may be some theatrics involved in you possibly adopting a different persona and behavior as the businessperson. Consider taking a program in theater.

CHAPTER 21

Future Forward

Highlights

Goal setting is all about managing your expectations. It is an exercise in wishful thinking, with a twist of ambition and avarice. It is a lot more interesting, creative, and fun than it sounds.

Managing expectations is an integral milestone in your journey toward making that "go/no go" start-up decision. Why? Because, once you set your goals, then you need to visualize and decide if those goals can and will be met. Are they too aggressive? Possibly unattainable? Or too conservative and need some punching up?

Regardless, the achievability of your goals, both business and personal, will be strategic determinants in your "go/no go" decision making awaiting you just down the road.

*Start with a simple bird's-eye view of both your **business** and **personal** goals.*

Business	Personal
Will business fulfill your entrepreneurial aspirations?	What are your goals in life (i.e., freedom, self-reliance, independence, wealth)?
What do you hope entrepreneurship will deliver for you (short, medium, and long term)?	Do you feel you have the wherewithal, staying power, ambition, and personal motivation to take on the challenge?
Where do you want to be "x" years from now? Can you see yourself at the helm of the company as it grows and matures?	What is your hopefully achievable goal for your family?

Tips for Goal Setting

- Set your start-up targets within your comfort zone and then reach a bit more. Any massive unreachable goals will cause frustration.
- There is a well-cited acronym that describes the best features of goals. It is called SMART (goals need to be *s*pecific, *m*easurable, *a*chievable, *r*elevant/reasonable, and bound by a "get it done" *t*imeframe). This offers you a useful benchmark in your goal-setting task.
- Set goals that are not overly complicated.
- Don't let others set your goals for you. They are yours and yours alone.
- Take baby steps, but never stop moving forward.
- Second-guessing is dangerous. It causes planning insecurities.
- We all have a built-in protective fear-or-flight reflex that safeguards us from harm. Knowing this in advance, try controlling its impact on your decision making. It can skew your direction.
- It's fine to carry out market research. It's harmful to compare yourself to others who have been in the game much longer. I did that when I started my consulting company, yardsticking myself to everyone in the field. It was demotivating.
- Getting discouraged is part of the game. You will likely get into trouble somewhere along the way. Make it your goal to look at every roadblock as a temporary challenge and not a permanent impediment.
- Learning from your experience, from others, from role models, and from others' successes and failures should be primary business goals. Why reinvent the wheel?
- Make a promise to yourself never to beat yourself up.

Goal setting comprises six building blocks made up of business and personal goals. Here are some examples of each. These are not suggestions, simply illustrations.

	Business Goals and Expectations	Personal Goals and Expectations
Short term (up to six months)	Secure investors or partners	Camper van for family get-away excursions
Long term (within "x" years)	XX% market share and multiple locations	Extended vacations, purchase villa in Italy
Life goals (the stuff dreams are made of)	Ability to build and sell my business	Retirement and freedom while I am still young

Hurdles

Goal setting requires introspection, best done in a setting free of distraction. Living on the West coast, my goal setting was always done while wandering in solitude, on a quiet beach, free of day-to-day distractions.

There is also often a malaise and insecurity in setting goals where you might think "I don't deserve that. I can't have that as my goal." My response to you would be that goal setting is an opportunity to create a wish list, and unless your aspirations are outrageous or "over the top" extravagant, then I respond "yes, you do deserve it."

Tales From the Trenches

I went through a goal-setting "exercise" with a bright, young tech entrepreneur whose reputation was gaining traction in the marketplace. His success seemed assured.

However, when it came to crystal ball gazing, he was lost. So much so that he asked his friends, family, and associates what his goals should be. I did not know he was doing this.

He presented me with a set of goals that were way out of character. He was obviously gullible and lost and had some flamboyant sources feeding him their own delusions. They were not taking his goal setting seriously.

I put a quick stop to that nonsense.

Together we set up a series of goal-setting sessions starting with short term. These were far easier for him to visualize. We did not move onto longer-term goals until he owned the more immediate ones that were within his reach.

Action Planning/Workbook

1. Set your business and personal goals with a maximum of five per line item (anything more is just too "all over the map" unattainable.

2. Review them all one more time. Now prioritize your goals within each category.

3. Discuss your business goals with a trusted business mentor/planner. Are your goals deemed viable and doable?

4. Discuss your personal goals with your partner/family. Gage how these goals are likely to be achieved and if you will get the support you need. There needs to be a clear understanding that reaching those goals will take sacrifice. Is everyone on board?

5. Having carried out the above, gage how committed you are to your stated goals. Any items need tweaking?

6. Keep your goals in plain sight, always.

7. Life does not travel in a straight line. Things change, in you, and around you. Make a commitment to revisit your goals at least twice a year.

CHAPTER 22

Risk

Harnessing the Beast

Highlights

Risk is a beast that demands to be tamed. It is an integral part of entrepreneurship. You will need to develop "risk tolerance" before it becomes "risk *in*tolerance."

Since this Playbook is dealing with business start-ups and early-stage venture launches, the concept of risk tolerance becomes an important factor for you to identify and measure. If you find that your risk capacity is low, then it should and must logically impact your "go/no go" decision. Only you can decide.

You can have the greatest opportunity, but if you can't bring it to fruition because you question and agonize over every step along the way, including to the point of affecting your health and well-being, then perhaps being an entrepreneur is not for you.

But let's be positive, ok?

There are *two categories of risks: real and perceived.*

1. *Real risks* are measurable and usually have a mitigating course of action. They are manageable.
2. *Perceived risks* are the boogeyman. They have not yet materialized, but are the subject of continual consternation. It's the "what if" syndrome and can be quite harmful as they linger, seemingly forever, giving your mind little rest and your imagination a heck of a workout.

Here are some features/traits of the more risk-tolerant entrepreneur. See how many you recognize in yourself.

Is This You?	YES That's Me	That's NOT Me
Enjoys a challenge		
Unafraid to make mistakes		
Learns from mistakes and failures		
Handles surprises well		
Does not thrive on the acceptance by others		
Strong intuition, more often right than wrong		
Little second-guessing of yourself		
See yourself as "edgy," different from others		
Impatient with indecisive people		
Micromanage to assure everything is done right		
Big on predictions and outcomes		
Likes unique/unchartered waters ideas		
Responds to questions with facts or a best guess		
Can take on risk. Have a high-risk capacity		
Appetite for adventure		
Own your tasks and responsibilities		
Own your mistakes		

(Note: There should be more ticks in "That's Me" column than in "That's NOT Me." This would indicate that you are a rational risk taker with a perspective and attitude that can cope with tolerating risk.)

Hurdles

Risk is exacerbated by a number of factors, all of which you need to control. Otherwise your risk tolerance will be so low that the resulting stress will impact your ability to perform.

- **Greed**, as in pushing the boundaries of what your venture is designed to deliver.

- ***Impatience***, *a drive and desire to get your initiative on stream faster, which in itself, can be a source of risk.*
- *The **need for small victories**, pushing the boundaries to score points for yourself and others (i.e., investors, family) represents a formula for enhanced risk.*

The way to best manage your risk tolerance is to be diligent in limiting the risks you pile onto yourself.

Tales From the Trenches

When I built my multimillion-dollar fiber plant, the risks presented themselves everywhere and all the time. From engineering, technology, cost overruns, city zoning, environmental compliance, labor, safety and product development, to quality control and, well, I think you get it.

My goal was to worry less today than I did yesterday.

My risk tolerance became manageable when I took emotion out of the issues and problems that arose. They were not my fault. They were not personal affronts. They became challenges that had to be tackled and difficulties that needed resolution.

Manhandling risks and removing the personal stigma of blame makes risk tolerance more endurable.

Action Planning/Workbook

1. Measuring your risk tolerance is critical. How well do you think you handle risks?
2. List five situations where you handled risks well.
3. Now list five situations where risks got the better of you. What could you have done differently?
4. In your current or past business environment, what do you identify as the most impactful risks and how do you handle them?
5. Do you enjoy the challenge of dealing with issues, challenges, and problems? Explain and justify.
6. Do you tend to ignore problems, hoping they will disappear on their own? If so, why?
7. Do you avoid confrontations? If yes, then why?

CHAPTER 23

The Family as a Support Mechanism

Highlights

There was no meeting of the minds. My dad thought that I was slightly crazy to go into business on my own. Conversely, my mom couldn't be more supportive and encouraging. My sister and my friends thought it was very cool. I took the leap and never looked back.

Family and friends need to believe in you as the risk-taking entrepreneur and respect what you are doing. They are your personal cheerleaders.

As an entrepreneur, support from family gives you strength and unwavering conviction to tackle challenges knowing there is a "team of supporters" behind you.

Family ties represent a critical piece of your "go/no go" business launch thinking. That is why it is included in this Start-Up Junkie's Playbook. At some point in time, as you mull over your 30-step results and decide which way to go, you will need to gage whether family and friends have your back.

The tight embrace of those close to you makes everything more attainable. We all thrive on warm fuzzies.

As part of your introspection regarding family support, here are some tips and red flags:

- Look for contrasting levels of support from within the family. This kind of division puts even more pressure on you as the responsible protagonist.
- Remember that even business associates you felt were close will tend to drift toward the next shiny coin on the road when you cannot deliver anything they need. Once there is

nothing in your relationship for them, they may well fade into obscurity. This sounds bitter, but experience has shown me the fickleness of those I once considered close business friends. I have learned that a business friend is an associate, not a friend that can steadfastly be counted upon.

- Set goals of what you expect from family and what they can expect in return from you.
- Let your family be your alarm for when you trip, go off track, change your behavior, or show signs of stress and pressure. Heed their concerns.
- Risk intensifies on an upward trajectory. Somewhere along the climb there will likely be a "red line" at which point family support may waver. Your family will send you cues, and you had better pay attention.
- In good business times, family support is appreciated. In tough times, that support is life-saving.
- In an unsupportive family setting, everyone's insecurities and doubts will become yours. Learn to deflect.

Tales From the Trenches

At one point in my career, the economy took a major downturn, spiraling into a recession. My job was in danger of vanishing, as was the company I worked for.

With virtually nothing in the bank, I sent out a huge stack of ever-so-slightly embellished resumes, to no avail. There was nothing out there. In actual fact, the best job at the time was a "dehiring specialist." You know the kind. They waltz into a company with employee lists in hand, carry out a "painless" mass firing/downsizing, and then offer useless training for a new job when new jobs were ultra-scarce. All in all, painful PR (public relations) theatrics. A sad memory, but I digress.

I launched my business out of necessity. I consulted with family and friends and welcomed their overwhelming support. My immediate family hid their apprehension well and became my biggest fans.

I owe my entrepreneurial success to them. I never forget it, and I never let them forget it either. It is one of our strong bonds.

Hurdles

Frankly, going it alone, or against the wishes of your family, can often increase your insecurities and put an end to your business dreams. An unsupportive or ambiguous family environment detracts from your ability to perform. Or, worse yet, forces you to settle for less.

Action Planning/Workbook

1. Start with your immediate family. Call for a get-together and explain your business opportunity and plans to launch your entrepreneurship voyage. Make sure they understand your reasoning behind it.
2. Let them speak, ask questions, state their concerns as they see them.
3. Respond to each and every issue they raise, and do so truthfully.
4. If there is a general consensus of support, let them know what you hope and expect from each of them. It could be volunteer help as you may need it or raiding the family piggy bank for some extra equity.
5. If there is resistance, find out why and what, and whether the issues can be addressed and remedied. If there is no resolution, you need to make a personal decision as to whether you want to proceed completely on your own or not and what backlash the lack of family support can create.

CHAPTER 24

Money, Money, Money

Highlights

Nothing happens in business without money, yours or OPM ("other people's money"). The poor dream about it. The rich yawn and take it for granted. And the businessperson sniffs and seeks it out.

There is an interesting exchange from *The Aviator* movie. When the young Howard Hughes was asked about his plans to build the greatest airplanes, he responded that all it took was money. The very wealthy host responded with "We don't talk about money here," to which Howard Hughes' response was, "Because you have it."

Money is a primal driver of business. Accessing money raises a number of questions for you, the would-be or early-stage entrepreneur. These questions will also help you when you reach that eventful "go/no go" crossroads.

Let's take a walk through the money minefield. Please answer the following questions.

Hopefully the results will fill you with confidence that money will not be a stumbling block for launching your venture... or it may be.

Either way, knowing where you stand will definitely decide if and when you launch your business and how grand an inauguration you can entertain.

Money, Money, Money	Yes	No
Do you expect to be profitable within six months?		
Do you have an effective, tested investor presentation? A Pitch Deck (a PowerPoint presentation package)?		
Can you justify all your numbers to tough financial managers?		
How long will it take your business to reach minimal profitability?		
How much do you need for prelaunch start-up costs?		

(*Continues*)

(Continued)

Money, Money, Money	Yes	No
How much cash flow is needed if you have to run six months with little revenue?		
What is your break-even level?		
What is your burn rate?		
Do you have personal funds to invest?		
If you are not 100% self-financed, where will you get your funding?		
What do you have to offer as security?		
Will offering security represent a risk for you, especially if you default?		
Have you spoken with any investors or strategic partners?		
How much equity do others want in your business?		
Have you researched any available grants for your business?		
Did you consider, or have you already presented at, an Angel Forum which is geared for start-ups/newbies to present to investors all looking for that next Steve Jobs?		
Is crowdfunding a potential for you?		
Do you recognize the difference between "venture capital" and "vulture capital"? If not, please research this before taking on investors		
When outside funding runs out, what then? Any provisions made? Plan B?		

If you don't have the answers to all of these, then please, please find out.

Hurdles

The worst feature of fundraising is that it is time consuming. You cannot spend all your time chasing money at the expense of your planning, launching and running your business.

In dealing with funders, it is common that those with money become the parents in a parent–child relationship where the parent takes on the dominant role. It becomes an uneven playing field. The entrepreneur needs to make an effort to keep the interaction on an even (parent–parent) footing.

Tales From the Trenches

Beware of the "investment ratchet clause." This is a mechanism whereby investors can be awarded additional equity in your company should you underperform based on predetermined deliverables.

A junior gold mining company I knew of, in desperate need of funds for exploration, secured such a questionable investment whereby the agreement demanded certain gold finding yields within a short period of time, just as the mining company promised.

Or else the investors were granted additional voting share equity in the company for every month the gold yield results did not materialize. Within a short period of time, the founders lost control of the company.

In an ironic twist, the Alaska-based gold mine uncovered a rich vein within two months of the founders ceding control.

Action Planning/Workbook

1. There are a series of questions in this chapter, each of which asks for a "yes" or "no" response from you. Go through them carefully and respond accordingly.
2. Any "no" answers represent a potential gap in your funding strategy that you will need to address. Tweak your pitch accordingly to avoid hearing "no."
3. Create a Pitch Deck about your business with the idea of attracting funders and investors.
4. Test the presentation with associates before you use it with funders.

CHAPTER 25

Your Business Model

Highlights

You have now come to the point whereby the bits and pieces of your research, planning, and financial projections, as represented in your proposed start-up business, will be tested. Prepare to justify and defend your entrepreneurial inspiration.

The next few steps can be described as "prepping for your go/no go" decision by diving deep into your business opportunity, how (and if) it would work, your risks and rewards, and how to make it happen. That's called your "**Business Model**."

You are approaching your crossroads, but you are not quite there yet. A little more mental gymnastics is needed. Sorry.

Your **Business Model** needs to answer some simple but critically important questions, like these:

- Will your business work?
- How will it work?
- Are you comfortable with your profit margins and markups?
- For product-oriented businesses, do you have multiple and reliable supply chains?
- Will there be sufficient cash flow to operate? To pay yourself?
- Who will do what? Do you need to hire staff? Will you contract out certain expertise like marketing or bookkeeping? You really don't have to do everything yourself.
- Can you bear up to the onslaught that competitors will throw your way, such as a barrage of discounts, sales, and market retention/protection strategies?
- Will your target audience respond to your efforts?
- Have you chosen the right customer base to pursue?

- Is your business sufficiently attractive to woo investors or traditional funders? What's in it for them? Hint—returns are a prime consideration, followed by an exit strategy at multiple times their original investment.

Which Business Model Do You Fit Into?

Where you fit influences how you operate and in what sphere(s) you circulate. Understanding your model will help round out the features and workings you build into your venture.

Business to business	Transactions take place between two or more businesses who may then distribute your products to lower-rung distributors or to resellers
	A loyal client following provides greater market predictability and stability than the other business models
Business to consumer	Your business sells directly to consumers who are the end users of your products or services
	Competitively low prices are keynote and characteristic in this model
	One of the major benefits of this model is that you can data-mine by collecting customer profiles and contacts, and use that data for future product/service development or for marketing initiatives
	Some companies, as we know, rent out these client lists to earn additional revenues. While this is commonplace, it is a questionable, gray area
Subscription based	Generally, applies if you sell software, newsletters, or any other service where the users pay a monthly or annual subscription fee to be part of the club. Health clubs are another example of this model
	Revenues are an "annuity," providing regular and predictable income
	Growth is experienced when new subscription signups outnumber those clients leaving you
On demand	Booking services represent applications of the on-demand model. Vacation travel booking companies such as Expedia, Travelocity, Airbnb, and Hotels.com are prime examples

	Entertainment streaming providers have fine-tuned this model, with great success
	Services such as technical support or health care websites answer questions on a user-fee basis
	In effect, any time an on-demand-for-pay business receives queries or demands of any kind, they fall within the scope of this model

Hurdles

The questions posed herein, and in the subsequent several probing chapters, demand attention and scrutiny. The responses you give form the foundational lifeblood of your new venture.

Further, once you commit your business to a specific Business Model, it may be difficult to shift to another. There is very little compatibility between models. Your customer base may not be transferable either.

Tales From the Trenches

A business client of mine was young, dynamic, and brilliant. His one major flaw was that he was dangerously arrogant, rendering him entrepreneurially oblivious. His business instincts cowered behind his unwavering belief that he was a winners' winner.

Actually, he invented the perfect "gizmoid" for a market that had no use for or interest in it.

When I questioned him as to who should or would buy his invention, he stated, confidently, that everybody needed one.

In fact, sales were so low that one of his largest operating expenses was warehousing his finished inventory.

I quizzed him endlessly, playing the devil's advocate. I constantly ran up against his protective wall of all-knowing arrogance. I needed to deliver a wakeup call to him.

"What happens when the money runs out and no investor or funder will touch you?"

Silence.

That was the clincher. We restarted his mentoring from the very beginning, not terribly different from the 30-step Playbook herein.

I found a fit for his invention elsewhere, not as a stand-alone item, but as a unique add-on building block within a multinational's family of products. It was a win–win. A Licensing Agreement was negotiated and my ecstatic client bought a piece of paradise somewhere and continues to happily tinker in his lab. My fees made the whole experience very tolerable, I might add.

Action Planning/Workbook

1. Decide very carefully which Business Model your business fits into.
2. Structure your operations, marketing, cash flow, and Strategic Planning around your Business Model. *Don't drift.*
3. Until the time that you launch your business and watch it flourish, remain diligent in your thinking. You need to be asking yourself: Will my business work? How will it work? What are the biggest impediments I need to overcome? and the entire gamut of "what if" questions and concerns that plague every fledgling business. *Start now.*

CHAPTER 26

Your Value Proposition

Highlights

Your **Value Proposition** sums up who you are and what you bring to the marketplace to meet customers' needs, or provides solutions to their problems. It exemplifies why you are in business. That having been said, what is a Value Proposition?

> Let's take McDonalds' Value Proposition as an example. The restaurant chain stands for "friendliness, cleanliness, consistency and convenience" as stated by its founder, Ken Croc. Its Value Proposition, however, is its convenience. That is what you know you're going to get when you go there. That exemplifies what McDonalds delivers to its customers.

As the start-up entrepreneur in the final stages of your "go/no go decision-making" journey, it is crucial that you understand and be acutely aware of exactly who you are, your place in the business food chain, and why you will (not should, but "will") meet your target audience's needs.

Your Value Proposition should express the very essence of your business that compels people to deal with you. It communicates to outsiders the reason you are in business, and make promises that you can and will deliver.

Building your Value Proposition on the backs of others by belittling competition is something companies often do. Please don't. Instead, focus on defining your own value for customers.

Fundamentally, you create a Value Proposition by following six steps:

1. Define your target audience, your core customers. By now you would have created a customer profile and have carried out sufficient market research to know your client base.
2. What brand messaging and marketing style will resonate with them?

3. Marry customer needs with your business's offerings. What are the customers' pain points? How will you help them solve problems or succeed in their own particular business?
4. Be specific about what you do or sell. No generalities, please. Nothing like "We offer solutions to industry's environmental concerns." More like "Our products can reduce your plants' emissions by as much as 20 percent." Capture their attention fast.
5. Is there anything unique about what you promote? If yes, your Value Proposition should emphatically draw attention to your innovation.
6. Test your Value Proposition with a "friendly business," that is, a prospective client with whom you have a working relationship. Pay attention to their reaction.

The *two main directions of Value Propositions* are (1) **gain creators**, namely how your product or service creates gains for the customer and (2) **pain relievers**, how your products or services alleviate clients' pain.

Which are you? Which are your products or services intended to concentrate on? Whichever best describes the results you intend to deliver needs to come across clearly and unequivocally in your Value Proposition.

Hurdles

If you can generate an effective Value Proposition, you are likely ready to move on to the next step in the 30-step process. If not, *do not pass Go, do not collect two hundred....* You really cannot make a "go/no go start-up decision" until you define yourself. Time to reaffirm who and what you are.

Tales From the Trenches

In my consulting practice, our core services were securing government grants for clients and/or connecting customers with investors, foundations, and other funding sources. This was what our clients expected from us, and this was what our reputation in the marketplace continually touted.

Grants were our primary focus. Our core Value Proposition tag line was "Nobody Hates Santa Claus." In a lighthearted way, it defined and identified us as the company that "helped deliver bags of money," that is, the Santa Claus people. It became the basis for our Marketing Strategy.

It spoke of gifts and goodies, all of which we delivered through our grant (and other funding) procurement services. That was what we were all about. Everybody knew it. It said it all.

Action Planning/Workplan

Respond to these questions. They will help you be clear on your all-important Value Proposition.

1. What is your Value Proposition? Define it until you believe it.
2. What exactly are you bringing to the market?
3. What do you want to be known for?
4. What do you want to be known as?
5. What are the products and/or services you offer and, most importantly, how do they meet the needs of your target audience?
6. Will your customers clearly understand your Value Proposition?
7. How compelling is your Value Proposition as compared to your prospective competitors? Are you different? Unique? Offering solutions that others do not?
8. Can you deliver your Value Proposition in a two-minute elevator pitch? If not, keep practicing.

CHAPTER 27

Your Business Plan Like No Other

Highlights

After you have successfully completed the laborious steps up to this point, congratulations are in order. So, my hearty congrats, but you're not quite done.

It's time for one final "kick at the can" in the form of a non-traditional Business Planning Checklist that ground-truths your business primarily to one person…you.

The following checklist encompasses highlights of everything you have researched, identified, and designed for your business initiative and *asks the simple question: "yes" or "no"?*

At this point, there is no room for "maybe" in your thinking.

It represents your final review before you would logically arrive at a "go/no go" decision as to whether to launch your business or look elsewhere for an opportunity.

Consider this your *Start-Up Junkie Challenge*.

This challenge will have three distinct objectives:

1. Identify any weaknesses in your planning, in which case you may want to revisit the gaps and fill the voids.
2. Provide the foundation for a traditional Business Plan for third parties such as funders, investors, and partners.
3. Most importantly, this checklist should give you, personally, a great deal more comfort and confidence in going forward with your business, should you decide to do so.

Business planning, particularly for start-ups, is a demanding taskmaster. It is unforgiving because you have so much at stake. This checklist is similarly demanding.

The **Start-Up Junkie Challenge** not only inquires about the results of your hardcore research and planning, but also delves into your personal space, the soft underbelly as to why you are doing this, your motivation, needs, and entrepreneurial makeup.

Start-Up Junkie Challenge	Yes	No
DREAMING AND SCHEMING		
The vision of your business is entrenched in your mind—perhaps not all the details quite yet, but certainly the broad strokes		
You think about it often, sometimes at the most inopportune times when your attention needs to be elsewhere		
Your business idea is something you feel pretty strongly is within your grasp to achieve		
The entrepreneur personality and character fits you. You wear it well. You are a free thinker and independent-minded		
You have a good idea of what it takes to bring the opportunity to fruition		
Prepared a personal inventory of what skills, experience, and industry knowledge you bring to the table		
THE FRENETIC SCRIBBLE		
Set up a tracking system to record and monitor the progress of your initiative. Create a visual vision board		
Carrying out weekly reviews of your progress and project evolution		
FLESHING IT OUT		
Early-stage analysis to determine if business is actually feasible and identify gaps and flaws in your Business Model		
Pros and cons list of the business idea's strengths and weaknesses		
Executive overview created including why you think it will work and why you feel there is a need		
Why you think you are the best person to run it		
YOUR FIRST SOUNDING BOARD		
Identified a third-party arms-length person who will act as an impartial and fearless sounding board		
PowerPoint Deck populated with the best-selling features of your opportunity		
Carried out presentation and discussions with sounding board mentor		
THE FEEDBACK FALLACY		
Designed and carried out focus group to garner feedback on your business concept and its viability, perceived market needs, and operating model		

Start-Up Junkie Challenge	Yes	No
MINDSET AND COMMITMENT		
List of five positive and negative features to describe your motivation to stick to this venture launch		
Five goals in your life and how committed you are to each, and how they relate to the business venture you are thinking of implementing		
WHY IS NOBODY ELSE DOING THIS?		
Revisited your Business Model and preliminary market research to identify why the field of competition is shallow		
Developed a "unique selling proposition" as to how you differentiate yourself with others and how your business can offer a competitive edge		
HELP ME MR. GOOGLE		
List of all the things about your venture that you are not certain about, potential gaps, and gray areas for further research		
Market research using all web platforms and identify useful, current market stats and trends and predictions for the future growth (or decline) of the marketplace		
UNDERSTANDING YOUR COMPETITORS		
Developed a clear profile and understanding of your competitors, their target markets, client profiles, Business Model and areas where you will compete, and also those features you have determined which will give you an edge		
Role model competitors with deep diving market research		
Placed yourself on competitors' market mailing lists and joined industry or trade association(s)		
FAD OR TREND		
Proof positive that your business opportunity is not a short-term flash fad		
WHO WILL BUY THIS?		
Crafted a customer profile with sufficient depth as to be able to design a market strategy to capture new clients		
THE DEEP DIVE INTO COMPETITION RESEARCH		
SWOT analysis of key competitors		
Determination of where you would have a distinct advantage, and what that might represent, and how to build on it		
GROWTH STRATEGIES		
Where do you hope to be three years downstream?		
How you envision reaching your goals		
Timelines and milestone chart to plot your growth strategy		
THE JOYS OF BRANDING		
Designed a brand for your business		
Tested the effectiveness of your brand with outside parties' feedback		

(Continues)

(*Continued*)

Start-Up Junkie Challenge	Yes	No
Created a message and tag line that would exemplify who and what you are		
Generated a memorable logo and tested it with other arms-length parties		
CAPTURE CUSTOMERS		
Created a "Customer Attraction Battle Plan"		
NUMBERS CRUNCHING: FUN WITH NUMBERS		
Designed a forecast model where you can comfortably support all the assumptions built in		
Ability to support debt as demonstrated in your cash flow		
Calculated burn rate and break-even analysis as additional support for your proforma forecasting		
START-UP COSTS		
Identified all your start-up costs, both soft costs and hard assets. Financial needs for your start-up have been identified, including cash flow for start-up period of six months following the launch		
Have a contingency for "miscellaneous" and "surprises"		
Comfortable that your start-up budget is sufficient		
Location of the business selected?		
PAUSE FOR A CHECKUP		
Completed and are satisfied with your responses in the "food for thought" checklist		
Revisited and tweaked any items identified as gaps		
REGULATORY, LEGALITIES, AND LICENSING		
Identified all the regulatory, licensing, and certification agencies whom you need to deal with		
Connected with all such agencies to assure there are no pending roadblocks that could endanger or decelerate the launch of your venture		
A VERY PERSONAL PERSPECTIVE		
Reviewed and scored the characteristics and personality traits of great entrepreneurs to gage which of those you exhibit		
Taken a clear inventory of what you bring to the table as far as passion and confidence, and being a self-starter		
FUTURE FORWARD		
Identified five top personal achievable goals		
Family support for your personal goals in place		
Identified top five achievable business goals		
RISK TOLERANCE		
List of five expected business risks compiled		
Mitigating strategies for anticipated business risks thought out		
Ability to handle risk as part of your character		

Start-Up Junkie Challenge	Yes	No
FAMILY		
Family briefed on your business venture, expected outcome, demand on your time, pain points expected during the journey		
All issues discussed thoroughly		
Family support confirmed and in place		
MONEY, MONEY, MONEY		
Funding sources identified		
Funding initial meetings and presentations carried out		
YOUR OPERATING MODEL		
Business Model fleshed out and detailed		
VALUE PROPOSITION		
Target audience identified		
Analysis of how your products/services solve customers' problems and meet their needs		
Your Value Proposition formulated?		
Your Value Proposition compared to competitors?		

I fully recognize that you completing this *Start-Up Junkie Challenge* has been an arduous and demanding task. My congratulations on your fortitude.

Your adherence to each of the steps outlined in this Playbook reflects your drive and motivation to pursue your entrepreneurial planning journey.

The attention you have paid to the "action planning/workplan" within each chapter is a testament to your commitment to being in business.

The assumption at this point is that you have earned a passing grade by responding "yes" to the above, and for those with an answer "no," you are in the process of scurrying back to fill any potentials gaps and voids.

Let's move on. The finishing line is within sight.

CHAPTER 28

You and Your Devil's Advocate

Your completed **"Start-Up Junkie's Challenge"** can now be scrutinized by a no-nonsense mentor/devil's advocate who must be given carte blanche to probe, question, and debate the key elements of your proposed business opportunity. Be confident. Encourage them to challenge you.

Find someone you trust but cannot influence. No bully tactics, please.

The reasoning for this last step is that, presumably, you have done everything possible to assess every aspect of your proposed business, including questioning your own motives and capabilities. But we all have a tendency to wear blinders that shield us from what we do not want to see or acknowledge.

You have a great deal at stake. This demanding confrontation is worthwhile.

Business is a gamble. This Playbook (and Workbook) has increased the odds that you will succeed. Notwithstanding all your efforts, there is still a risk involved.

One final look-through is highly recommended. You need a fresh pair of eyes.

The Role of the Devil's Advocate

- The role of the devil's advocate is that of a contrarian, offering alternate views on what you deem as accurate and correct.
- Focuses on sound opinions. Provides solid logic and rationale.
- Takes an opposing vantage point to yours which forces you to defend your position.
- Tests the strength of your arguments.

- The actions of the advocate will help create a stronger Business Model with less gaps and more punch.
- If you have separate devil's advocates, say one each for marketing, funding, and operations, you will have access to each one's specialized areas of expertise.
- Pushes you to explain and justify your position and assumptions.

There are, however, disadvantages to using a devil's advocate.

- You might become too argumentative and couch your responses in irrational and emotional overtones.
- You might lose some of your motivation to move forward, or the advocate debate itself will cause delays and disruptions.
- All care must be exercised to assure that the discourse between the devil's advocate(s) and yourself is productive, with mutual respect governing the interaction.

Undertake this step in the spirit of positiveness and good faith.

CHAPTER 29

More Tales and Lessons From the Trenches

Hands-on experiences teach us as only forays into the real world can do. They are not part of an academic "how to" textbook. They serve as invaluable business mentoring sessions on what to do, what not to do, and how different scenarios play out when real-time outcomes are at stake.

That is why each chapter of this Playbook contains "Tales From the Trenches" as illustrations of where I personally have succeeded, or failed, or just witnessed magic moments when everything came together, or flew off into oblivion. Hopefully these "Tales From the Trenches" have added to your experience.

But there's more. Always more stories, each one teaching us a lesson.

Just before you are called upon to cast your "go/no go decision," I would like to share several more instances where business works, or backfires. Regardless, each incident can make you a more capable and savvier businessperson. That is the intent.

Hanion's Razor: "Never Attribute to Malice That Which Is Adequately Explained by Stupidity"

I had a competitor who was fiercely jealous of the inroads I had made with my consulting firm. Aside from trying (and failing) to poach my clients (formerly his clients), he came after me full-on.

He complained about me to everyone he met. He wrote nasty letters to event organizers where I was scheduled to speak or chair a discussion panel. He would attend any event where I was giving an address so that he could pose probing questions that generally had little to do with my presentation. He was like a walking, talking National Enquirer.

He plagiarized huge excerpts of my published works and took full credit for them. He literally "borrowed" several complex economic models I had developed for several government economic ministries, took full credit (naturally), and, with little understanding of how to apply and decipher these models, used them in his own reports. It was laughable, and everybody knew it.

I had long ago decided not to pursue him since his libelous and self-destructive behavior was the best advertising I could ask for.

It was the manner in which he seemingly tried to undo me. It was a blatant and childish power trip. It did nothing to build his own practice. In fact, he was committing the fundamental error of trying to build up and promote his business on the backs of his competition. Me.

Eventually he moved on. I purchased his customer base and a few other resources he had developed, some of which were twins to my own. It did not cost much to do so. It was almost an act of mercy.

The lesson here: Watch out for the other kids in the playground, especially the bullies and the ones jealously eyeing your toys.

The Knock-Off Chinese "iPadd"

One of my mandates was to attend a foreign technology products trade fair and search out new products for my North American client. I was a tech lover and aficionado. Imagine being paid to play with the latest gizmos! It was heaven.

At one booth, sponsored by an Asian manufacturing company, there was a display of very inexpensive tablets, many of which sported a bastardized Apple logo.

I picked one up to examine it. The label read iPadd. This was not a spelling error.

"What's this?" I inquired.
"It's an iPadd" was the answer.
"You spelled it wrong," I said.
"No, we didn't. It's our iPadd."
"You even have the Apple logo on it."

"No, it's our logo. See? No bite out of the apple."

I was enthralled. Here I was holding a knock-off iPad that was over an inch thick, and with an operating system that allowed you to go get a coffee while it whirled and loaded any program.

"This operating system is slow. What is it?"

"OSS" was the response. "We developed it."

Nothing further needed to be added.

He then proceeded to load a kind of Angry Birds game, but they looked more like angry vultures.

"How much for the iPadd?" I asked.

"Ninety-nine U.S. dollars."

I was floored. "Any guarantee?"

"Replacement. You ship it back to Shenzhen, China and we will
  replace it."

I pulled out my own iPad (one "d" only) and showed it to him. He remained oblivious.

The sales rep was obviously sold on his iPadd.

Blind belief out of necessity ruled the day. If often does.

Don't Ask Me to Sign Anything

I once had a partner in a business, or I think he was a partner, but we had no signed agreement. He wouldn't sign anything.

Although I thought that was odd, I was blinded by the profit potential of the initiative, as sold to me by Mr. Invisible, as I began to call him.

I queried him about that, and he always responded in a somewhat joking manner, making obscure references to this and that. My level of suspicion grew daily.

One day, we needed to submit a series of signed documents to an investment group interested in our venture. Mr. Invisible was nowhere to be found, even though he knew the offer had a time limit.

"You sign it," he texted me. "I am gone for a few days," apparently returning after the due date for submitting the paperwork. I did not submit, and he was livid. I did not budge.

This was a perfect opportunity to confront him on his bizarre behavior. Pot of gold returns or not, all my Spidey-senses were tingling.

The truth came out. It was a tale of why never to partner with a crook. His story included a vicious divorce and an ex-wife stalking him, a previous business deal (or two or three, never got the exact numbers) where ex-partners were legally pursuing him, and a gambling addiction that came with some loansharking issues.

I dissolved the company and walked away amidst his threats. The way I saw it, there were enough people on his trail that our brief encounter would disappear into oblivion.

Did I mention never to deal with crooks? If there is any jittery uncertainty on your part, walk away. Protect your assets and your reputation, which are priceless.

"Broken Telephone" Presentations

I had a speaking engagement in Tianjin, China, extolling the virtues of investing in Western United States and Canada. It was a glamorous affair, and addressing the thousand or so attendees was an experience.

The event planners judiciously upgraded my PowerPoint to include Chinese text.

My translator kept up with my presentation pace. I never liked working with translators because it can be a case of "broken telephone." The message can get lost.

In the question and answer period, the audience which was composed of many "young Asian investor bulls" spoke perfect English.

In subsequent speaking engagements in a foreign setting, I would ask my assigned event translator to draft (in writing) my presentation into his language. Then I would take that and have an independent translator read it back to me in English. I wanted to assure that my message was not mangled.

I actually followed this same process if and when there was a deal structured with a foreign party. All non-English Agreements, Memorandums of Understanding, and NDAs were translated back to English for me by several independent interpreters.

Please Join My Board of Directors

I had a business associate and good friend who was far smarter than me. He often invested in "bleeding-edge" businesses which developed technologies or biotechnologies beyond the comprehension of the common person. Certainly, beyond mine.

In one instance, he founded a company whose Intellectual Property baffled me. I could not grasp how it worked or how the world would benefit from its presence. No explanation on his part penetrated my ability to grasp the concept. It was an ordeal for him to explain and extoll the brilliance of his latest "baby," and watch me squint and squirm as he spoke.

(Apparently, squinting does not increase your ability to embrace something that is beyond you. I should have remembered that from school.)

"Come sit on our Board," he said. "But, but, but…" was my response.

"It doesn't matter. In fact, it will do us good to have an ignorant Board Member. Join because you obviously know nothing." I qualified.

It actually made sense. I was the "common man" sounding board they needed to convert. It was a marvelous experience, and a great lesson in humility.

I Want to Sell to All of China

In one of my workshops, I tossed out the question "Who will you sell to?" One answer from an enthusiastic young entrepreneur was "China."

Having just completed a magazine article on doing business in China, my response was "Which one of the 23 massive and demographically unique provinces and 1.4 billion people spread out over four million square miles are you referring to?"

Silence prevailed.

It has always been my contention that you need to identify and work to capture a target audience of customers/clients within a target market place. When that is done and you have reached a certain capacity of users, only then can you move on.

Focus, people, focus.

What's a Fair Price to Charge?

In cases where your business is knowledge or service based, setting prices can be somewhat of a challenge. Quite often, clients are paying you for what or who you know, where the fees are not governed by the more traditional methods such as using per diem rates.

Case 1: The Bill Bully

I had a client who needed a personal introduction to someone who could help him land a contract. Just an introduction. Despite all his own efforts, he never made it past the contact's gatekeeper, Executive Assistant.

I knew the contact and the gatekeeper well and agreed to arrange the introduction for a large fee. It was a totally arbitrary price since my effort would be comprised of one telephone call, maybe two. It worked.

Through this new liaison, my client was able to get onto a bidders list for a multimillion-dollar contract which he won. But he was unhappy with me. My fees, according to him, were excessive for the actual effort it took me.

I smiled the kind of forced smile you wear when you have slammed your fingers in the door, and explained slowly so as not to show my frustration that I was being paid for what and who I knew and was not "punching a clock." I then added, jokingly, that I would gladly replace my original invoice and just invoice him for a percentage of the contract he had won. The amount of my invoice would be five times my original agreed-upon price.

I was paid, reluctantly, but it did not end there. I endured a dressing-down session every time I met the client at a conference. Interestingly, he never shied away from recommending me to his business associates. Go figure.

My takeaway lessons were simple: (1) learn to invoice in advance for all or most of your intended work, and (2) never succumb to "bill bullies."

Case 2: The Grateful, Appreciative Client

In another instance, there was an investment deal almost on the table for my aging client. He was selling his business because of ill health. His daughter was not well either. I had grown very fond of the family during the backs-and-forths of the negotiations.

The impediment to the deal was my fees which skewed the selling price beyond the business's valuation.

I just personally wanted my client and his family to succeed. I agreed to forego my fees entirely out of the deal, and the buyout was successfully concluded. Nothing left on the table for me, but I was okay with that.

Several weeks later, I was surprised when I received a very heart-felt thank you card from the seller and his whole family, along with a generous check, and a basket of his wife's homemade cookies.

Luckily, you will encounter more clients like this one and less "bill bullies."

This sharp contrast of scenarios also led me to start screening my prospective clients as closely as they scrutinized me.

After all, good business should be a mutual affair.

Hidden Depth of Knowledge

I once was part of a joint venture in St. Petersburg (Russia). It was a massive lithium battery company that covered three square city blocks.

My associates and I saw this as a golden opportunity since the advent of high-storage car batteries was the coming trend.

The plant was built in Stalin's time, and likely manufactured some nasty weapons over the decades. However, with Glasnost came the need to find new products, since the almost-bankrupt Russian government had no funds to support the factory and its several thousand workers.

The plant was in disrepair with peeling linoleum flooring, lots of unused and discarded antiquated equipment, and a relative hodgepodge of products being produced, including lapel pins and metal rulers. What a horrific, degrading shift it must have undergone after years as a military parts producer. But what they did have was electric battery Intellectual Property.

Their latest revenue-generating endeavor was rechargeable batteries of all kinds, from button cell batteries to massive mobile power plants.

The Russian work ethic at the time was lax, with an unwillingness to look beyond the drab. Change was not encouraged. What a waste.

The place was like Willie Wonka on drugs. There was no sense of efficiency or production flow management. The workers were there to loiter with a smidgen of toil in the mix, while waiting for the paymaster's truck to arrive loaded with Rubles.

By North American standards, it was all laughingly absurd.

But there was a spark. The knowledge base was well educated, creative, but, unfortunately, stifled in their resolve to institute change. These were good people in a bad place. We were determined to let them shine.

We engaged with the inventors, engineers, designers, and forward-thinkers. They were our reason for staying involved.

We further instituted North American production training for the workforce and managed to ever-so-slightly instill a work ethic. It was a foothold.

Over time, we brought production orders to the plant: titanium machinery parts, power stations, consumer and industry lithium battery product needs, and more. And once the factory started generating activity beyond CCCP memorabilia label pins, the plant just seemed to come to life.

Unfortunately, once the joint venture began to show a profit, the Russian Mafia (jokingly referred to as the "Russian Economic Wealth Redistribution Group") took control and generously bought us all airline tickets to get the hell out.

The lesson here is know who you are crawling into your business bed with. If you "peel back the layers of the onion," as the expression goes, there should be no signs of infestation.

I Almost Met Pamela Anderson

Years ago, I had a bright young filmmaker as a client. Over a year or two, I helped him secure funding to grow his fledgling business and to produce an independent film. It was a most pleasant relationship and taught me about a sector I was not very familiar with.

As it happens, he also produced some commercial work. I followed his career as he developed into a sought-after writer and producer.

On one occasion, he had an assignment to film Pamela Anderson who was promoting her PETA involvement. Here was my chance for payback.

I asked for an invitation to be on set. "No. It's a closed set" was the response. "Well, how about as a lighting tech or production assistant?" I joked. "Can't do it" was the response.

I was crestfallen. My *Baywatch* heroine was so close, yet so far.

In business networking and relationship building, there is always the expectation of a two-way street and the sharing of opportunities. Apparently not always so.

"Give" but don't always expect to "get." That's the takeaway.

Sorry, Pamela. I was ready and able.

CHAPTER 30

Go/No Go?

There comes a time between
turning the page
or closing the book

—Bob Seeger

It's time! You have arrived at the "go/no go" decision crossroads. But that doesn't mean you have to jump right away. Window of opportunity time permitting, put everything away for a few days or a week or more before deciding. This is a big decision.

One of the scariest things is that, regardless of how much market research and analysis you have done, you will never have enough information. You will be making a decision based on what you have compiled. That's just a reality.

Here are a few tips on the act of making decisions that can change the course of your life:

- Review all your responses to the host of "checkups" and checklists in this Playbook. They should have proved useful in solidifying your ideas (or demanding greater due diligence).
- Have your closest business associate prepare a list of the toughest questions they can think of. Your job is to respond effectively.
- Avoid "decision fatigue" by making hard choices too quickly or spontaneously.
- Focus down on the important issues and try to discard the mounds of peripheral information and research you have accumulated in the process. Don't get bogged down.
- Step back to see the 50,000-foot view. The big picture of where this is going will help add perspective.

- Part of your decision will be guided by emotion and "gut feel." Pay attention. These are both safety nets.
- Run your final decision by those close to you or those who will likely be the ones impacted the most. Seek out the support and consensus that is offered.
- If you feel that you do not have all the information or options, then hold off and regroup.
- Imagine if you say "no go," what would the implications be? Life would go on, right? New opportunities may crop up too?
- Disassociate and switch teams. Put yourself in someone else's place. Perhaps you would be the person mentoring your doppelganger who, by no coincidence, wants to go into your business. You would be advising your twin on your business. What would you counsel them to do? "Go or no go"?
- Understand that your decision has long-term implications, but rarely irreversible. Business is not a life or death game. Don't freeze up in your decision making.

Entrepreneurial "Truisms" to Live and Die By

Since you are about to possibly embark on your entrepreneurial adventure, I felt compelled to offer up a Jambalaya of my real-world truisms, some achieved through my business successes and others revealed through growing pains, false starts, and trial and error. Everything is a learning experience.

Understanding and appreciating these will give you a head start to get to where you want to go. Just as importantly, **they will provide you with a greater perspective right here and right now in your "go/no go" decision making.**

1. Entrepreneurship is not a job. It's an identity, someone you become.
2. Don't overcomplicate. If your business venture requires four people at the table, don't send out 10 invitations.
3. Appreciate your business opportunity. Take nothing for granted.
4. Make very, very sure that someone will be willing to pay for what you want to sell. Never develop anything in a vacuum.

5. Understand your target customers' needs and fill them. Understand their problems, and offer solutions.

6. Don't "build it and they will come." That is the plot of a B-grade movie, not a business vision.

7. Know what you personally want out of life, what will make you happy. An unhappy entrepreneur is defeated right at the starting gate.

8. Expect imperfections along the road to perfection. And, incidentally, nothing is ever or will ever be perfect. Don't wait for perfection before you launch. You will likely get leapfrogged by competitors.

9. Overnight success takes time. Be patient.

10. Sidestep drama from friends and family. Don't get distracted.

11. Entrepreneurship is a mental game of stamina, resilience, and passion. It's a road trip. Check your gas tank.

12. Beta test, and do it early on. Don't wait for a "final product/service."

13. If you can avoid it, don't be a solopreneur. Share the load. Delegate. Contract or hire expertise and abilities that will free you up to focus on what you do best.

14. Switch places. Do some role-playing. Would you be your customer?

15. Treat everyone with respect. The person you snub may be the gatekeeper for the person you need.

16. Make friends. Make fans. Build loyalty. Every businessperson needs to surround themselves with followers.

17. Business ethics are a gray area. Be guided by right and wrong, but ultimately, your own judgment will determine the goalposts and the risks.

18. Hustling is not a dirty word. Sell, sell, sell. (No sales = no cash flow.)

19. Entrepreneurship creates imbalance. You will be out of balance just with the effort you are putting into the building process. Know, however, that, over time, it will eventually balance out.

20. Things change. Remain curious about everything: your market, competitors, industry trends, the level of satisfaction of your customers, and, of course, your very own business.

21. Don't spend like you have already made it if you haven't. Cash flow is a precious commodity in new and early-stage ventures.

22. Become a storyteller. Talk to people. Open up. Let outsiders in.
23. Lastly, have a "Plan B." There are always other opportunities out there for the trying and taking. Keep other potential business options and opportunities in abeyance, tucked away somewhere safe should you want to go there or need to pivot on your immediate plans.

There's no such thing as the unknown, only things temporarily hidden.
—Even Captain Kirk always had a "Plan B"

From one start-up junkie to another, I wish you the very best of luck.
—Jay J. Silverberg, Business Mentor and Author

APPENDIX 1

Glossary of Terms

Acting: when you need to take on a role or business persona different to your regular self; putting up a front; playacting.

Active Listening: the skill of paying attention to others when they speak or offer advice, and taking their input seriously.

Assumption: a piece of information or a statement made that you can back up; a truism; financial information in a forecast based on assumptions you make.

Brainstorming: a collection of minds contributing to a solution, design, or creation, offering different viewpoints to the same issue at hand.

Break Even: the revenues you need to generate to make zero profit or zero loss; the minimum business level you need to realize to stay afloat.

Burn Rate: Assuming you generate zero revenues, what are the cash flow expenses you need to cover to keep the lights on? A prominent question from investors.

Business Goal: targets you set to achieve, either personally, collectively, or corporate.

Business Model: a collection of strategies, operational and administrative issues that, combined, lay out the parameters of how you function.

Business Plan: a brain dump of information, analysis, and business modeling prepared for a specific target readership; possibly one of many written for the same business but for different audiences.

Change: how a person or business changes in light of direct and indirect influences, market and economic fluctuations, change in family status or pressures; becoming and acting differently.

Checklist: a set of items and tasks that need to be completed; a collection of "to do" items that demand your attention.

Client Profile: an assessment of your client's makeup, who they are, how they function, and primarily what they need and how you can provide that; a precursor to any meetings or sales efforts with clients; very client specific.

Competitive Analysis: finding out everything you can about your competitors; comparing your products/services/technology/selling points between yours and theirs.

Customer: your most important asset. It doesn't get any simpler than that.

Deliverable: as in delivering what you promise to a customer; a high level of performance.

Due Diligence: analyzing an item to the "n-th" degree; looking at something from every conceivable angle; the ability to conclude "yes, that makes sense."

Feasibility Study: a review of the economics and viability usually associated with a business or opportunity; how and if an idea can logically be implemented; the identified roadblocks to realizing an opportunity.

Focus Group: a collection of arms-length reviewers prepared to offer input, impressions, and preferences regarding an object, service, or concept, such as a business idea or brand.

Gap: a black hole in your thinking or assumptions; something demanding closer attention; a void.

Impact: a force or situation that influences another; the process whereby a design or concept is influenced by other sources; possible game-changers.

Initiative: a project or business; a start-up; a fledging; a thought that can mature into something real.

Life Cycle: period of time from inception to retirement or obsolescence.

Methodology: the definable process used to analyze and measure; explaining or justifying how you arrive at a decision

Model: as in "Business Model"; a representation of the workings of a business concept.

Monitor: to actively follow; measure changes; track progress and performance; provide the impetus for change.

Need: something that has a requirement; a problem or opportunity that demands to be addressed.

OPM: other people's money, as in accessing outside investors and funders for your business.

Pitch Deck: generally refers to a PowerPoint presentation designed specifically to "pitch" an idea or present to prospective funders and investors; also refers to a product or service being pitched to a client and often using PowerPoint as a marketing tool.

Plan: as in to lay out possibilities and options; as in "business planning."

Project: a temporary endeavor undertaken with the express intention of it possibly being implemented.

Real World: a phrase that implies that what is being discussed has roots in ordinary or everyday experiences; the ability to judge the reality of an idea or concept; ability to morph an idea into realistic implementation.

Risk: identifying possible outcomes to an action, or to inaction; the cost involved in investing time and money without carefully judging its chances of failure; a realistic analysis of prospective roadblocks and danger

SWOT: analysis and quantification of ideas or business concept's strength, weaknesses, opportunities, threats; the basis for big picture planning; taking an objective 50,000-foot view

Vulture Capital: a form of investment to avoid; there will be a clause in the agreement that you give up shares for every increment of revenue or profit targets you fail to achieve. Avoid this. It can be fatal!

APPENDIX 2

Location Selection Guide and Checklist

The location selection for your enterprise is an important consideration. It can make the difference between operating a profitable business or dealing with the shortcomings and challenges that a disadvantageous location can represent.

The following is a *Location Selection Guide and Checklist*. Please keep in mind that this is a comprehensive, all-inclusive checklist, and that not all items listed here may apply to your particular type of business.

Item	Description/Criteria	Yes/No?
Close to customers	It is important to try to locate close to your major customers. Not only does this keep shipping costs down, but it allows you to maintain a close contact with your customer base	
Rent costs	The most obvious area most businesses consider is the cost of the rent or lease (although it is only one consideration, as demonstrated in this checklist). Rent is often quoted by the unit or by the square footage. If you are signing a lease, please make sure it is for a term you can accept, for example, one to three years. It should have an "escape clause" if the landlord does not complete any repairs or changes to what he agrees to. You can also request one to three months free as part of your lease signing	
Worker safety	Standards (including regulatory) that need to be adhered to	
Property taxes	Property taxes, especially on commercial and industrial sites, can be a significant cost of your operations. Check with the municipality	

(Continues)

(Continued)

Item	Description/Criteria	Yes/No?
Insurance rates	Insurance should include business interruption, fire, theft, and liability. The rates will also be lower if you are close to a fire hydrant or if the location is sprinkler-protected	
Sprinklers	If your type of business requires sprinklers (as prescribed by law or regulation), make sure that is already in place. It is costly to get it installed yourself	
Competition cluster	Businesses that are alike tend to cluster together. That is particularly true about food, restaurants, car dealers, service depots, and so on. Clusters attract customers. If this "cluster" effect would serve your business well, then your location selection should consider this	
Infrastructure	Power, sewer, water, loading bays/shipping bays, and parking are all important considerations. For example, not all locations have 220-volt power that some equipment needs, and installing this yourself is very costly	
Close to highways	A business close to highways or highway access makes shipping easier and provides better access for suppliers, customers, and employees	
Technology	The location should have excellent high speed and/or optical cable serviced by one of the major providers	
Employees	You may want to assure that the location you choose is close to a ready pool of employees you may need for your business	
Subcontractors	Your business may require subcontractors or equipment-servicing companies. Make sure there are those necessary providers within your general location. The same applies to transport companies and other suppliers of parts or materials you may need	
Expansion room	It is prudent (but not always possible) to try to make sure there is room to expand as you grow. That means locating where you may be able to take an option for more space. The cost of moving is high	
Business license	This is a reasonable simple process, that is., getting a business license. However, make sure that the location allows a business such as yours to set up. There are often restrictions for manufacturing that create dust or smoke. There are also restrictions about traffic (in and out), parking, or the size of vans allowed in certain areas	

Item	Description/Criteria	Yes/No?
Regulatory	For anything where the final product will be consumed, there is a requirement for stainless steel processing and handling equipment, as well as regulations for staff clothing, hairnets, sanitation, and conforming with reporting and record-keeping	
Storage, warehousing	Your business may require storage of raw materials or finished products. In some cases, this can require a large space. The location you choose may need to include storage or warehousing	
Workshop area	If your business requires a workshop area or spray booth, for example, there are regulations about safety, materials handling, and ventilation	
Dust collection	If your business is manufacturing or if you will be creating dust or smoke, the location needs to have a dust collection/filtration system in place, or you will require permission to install one	
Signage	If you require visibility, make sure you are allowed (by the landlord and the local government) to put up signage, and check the maximum signage allowable. Each location has different regulations	
Other Nonphysical Location Options		
Virtual business	You may not require a physical space, just a cell-phone number, fax, website, social media page, or messaging center where customers can reach you. The mobile office is becoming a mainstay of today's entrepreneurial operations	
Business center	These are centers (locations) where you can rent a single office, but have access to meeting rooms, someone to answer your phone (and pass messages to you), and a place to meet customers.	
Home-Based Businesses		
Licensing	Your home-based business may require a business license. Your location may not be zoned for a home-based business. Check with the local authorities	
Safety	Liability insurance is important. If someone is injured at your location, or arriving to or leaving from your place of business, insurance coverage is vital This would include covering any potential liabilities where there is the possibility of damages	
Insurance	Sufficient insurance for your computer equipment, inventory, and any other pieces of equipment is important. Coverage is not expensive	

(Continues)

(*Continued*)

Item	Description/Criteria	Yes/No?
	Home-Based Businesses	
Dedicated space	Home-based businesses can often interfere with "home," that is, the living space of your family. It is best to try to dedicate space to your business, for example, a room, basement, garage, or separate building on your property	

About the Author

Jay J. Silverberg is a "business rebel" and start-up junkie who has started several successful businesses. As an entrepreneurial mentor, Jay has developed innovative programs and resource materials and inspired thousands of businesspeople, managers, and business instructors. As a business consultant, Jay's practice ranged from start-ups to Fortune 500 firms, with projects that have spanned the globe.

This is Jay's fourth book in the collection, joining *A Cynic's Business Wisdom: Winning Through Flexible Ethics*, *Dead Fish Don't Swim Upstream* (coauthored with Bruce McLean), and *Stuck Entrepreneurs: Escape Routes Out of The Quicksand*.

Jay welcomes feedback and inquiries. He can be contacted at silverberg88@gmail.com.

Index

OTHER TITLES IN THE ENTREPRENEURSHIP AND SMALL BUSINESS MANAGEMENT COLLECTION

Scott Shane, Case Western University, Editor

- *The Most Common Entrepreneurial Mistakes and How to Avoid Them* by Lisa J Peck-MacDonald
- *The Hybrid Entrepreneur* by Kevin J. Scanlon
- *Stuck Entrepreneurs* by Jay J. Silverberg
- *Teaching Old Dogs New Tricks* by Thomas Waters
- *Building Business Capacity* by Sheryl Hardin
- *The Entrepreneurial Adventure* by Oliver James
- *So, You Bought a Franchise. Now What?* by David Roemer
- *The Startup Masterplan* by Nikhil Agarwal and Krishiv Agarwal
- *Managing Health and Safety in a Small Business* by Jacqueline Jeynes
- *Modern Devil's Advocacy* by Robert Koshinskie
- *Dead Fish Don't Swim Upstream* by Jay J. Silverberg and Bruce E. McLean
- *Founders, Freelancers & Rebels* by Helen Jane Campbell
- *The 8 Superpowers of Successful Entrepreneurs* by Marina Nicholas
- *Navigating the New Normal* by Rodd Mann
- *Time Management for Unicorns* by Giulio D'Agostino

Concise and Applied Business Books

The Collection listed above is one of 30 business subject collections that Business Expert Press has grown to make BEP a premiere publisher of print and digital books. Our concise and applied books are for...

- Professionals and Practitioners
- Faculty who adopt our books for courses
- Librarians who know that BEP's Digital Libraries are a unique way to offer students ebooks to download, not restricted with any digital rights management
- Executive Training Course Leaders
- Business Seminar Organizers

Business Expert Press books are for anyone who needs to dig deeper on business ideas, goals, and solutions to everyday problems. Whether one print book, one ebook, or buying a digital library of 110 ebooks, we remain the affordable and smart way to be business smart. For more information, please visit www.businessexpertpress.com, or contact sales@businessexpertpress.com.

www.ingramcontent.com/pod-product-compliance
Lightning Source LLC
Chambersburg PA
CBHW061317220326
41599CB00026B/4919